Thinking for Results

Safer Schools and Higher Student Achievement

Donna Wilson, Ph.D.

&

Marcus Conyers

Authors: Donna Wilson, Ph.D. and Marcus Conyers
Layout design: Lorraine Holden
Cover/Interior graphics: Lorraine Holden
Editing: Jeanne Zehr and Dara Lee Howard

ISBN 1-58933-044-8

Contents

Chapter 1

The Astonishing Discovery

1

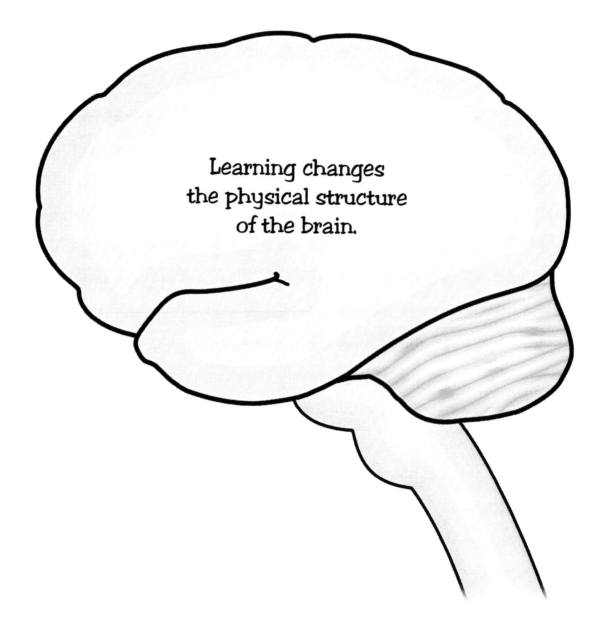

Learning changes
the physical structure
of the brain.

The Astonishing Discovery

Research suggests that learning changes the physical structure of the brain and that the capacity to think effectively can be learned (Branford et al., 1999). Furthermore, academic achievement is greatly influenced by students' abilities to apply thought processes in a systematic way.

Some students arrive at school with these cognitive assets in place. They have the capacity to benefit from standard teaching practice if they are motivated to do so. Other students do not arrive with all these assets in place. They may start school motivated but they quickly lose ground as their reading, writing, and computing skills fail to develop at the prescribed rate. One costly solution is to get them to repeat the grade, costing the taxpayer $4,000 to $12,000 while the student suffers the loss of self-belief the equivalent to becoming blind or losing a parent. Another solution is to cultivate the cognitive assets the students need to do well in school and in life so they can become positive, healthy, and productive citizens.

The Thinking for Results (T4R) approach focuses on cultivating cognitive assets in our students so that we can honestly move towards the mission "All students will be successful." One of the key components of the model is the Three Phase Cognitive Model, which centers on three components of purposeful cognition: gathering information; processing information; and applying information to achieve desired results. This approach supports academic achievement, encourages a safe school environment, and can be the framework for a lifetime of successful thinking.

Neurocognitive Plasticity

The National Research Council suggests that the physical structure of the brain *actually* changes when learning occurs. In the book *How People Learn* (Branford et al., 1999) they state the following: a) Learning changes the physical structure of the brain; b) Structural changes alter the functional organization of the brain - in other words, learning organizes and reorganizes the brain; and c) Different parts of the brain may be ready to learn at different times.

For the past 50 years, researchers and practitioners have been studying and using Reuven Feuerstein's theory of Structural Cognitive Modifiability (Feuerstein, Rand, Hoffman, & Miller, 1980). This theory states that the thinking capabilities of humans change as we learn. Furthermore, it also states that if students learn to learn with specific cognitive skills, they increase their ability to learn throughout life. As a school psychologist, Donna served more than 1,000 students by diagnosing and assessing their cognitive and affective skill development and student achievement level. She saw first hand the increases

3

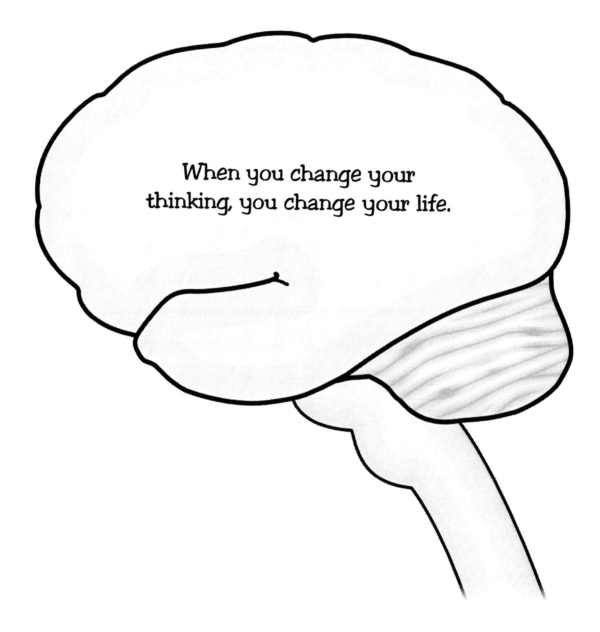

When you change your
thinking, you change your life.

in student performance that flowed from interventions that leveraged the marvel of neurocognitive plasticity. The theory of neurocognitive plasticity states that the capacity for the human brain to think, learn, and communicate can be enhanced through cognitive interventions that change the physical structure of the brain. The authors define neurocognitive plasticity as follows:

Neuro – Having to do with the central nervous system
Cognitive – The act or process of perceiving or knowing
Plasticity – Able to be molded or shaped

Examples Illustrating Neurocognitive Plasticity

Neurocognitive plasticity may affect all areas of life. Consider the following examples from research.

Reading – Low performing readers who receive 40 hours of intensive coaching can restructure their thinking so they can read on grade level (Allington & Cunningham, 1996).

Optimism – Children and adults who engage in specific cognitive interventions can move from an habitual negativistic thinking form to one that is more optimistic (Seligman, 1998).

Productivity at work – Employees who focus on developing certain cognitive assets can increase their productivity 100% to 400% (Kelley, 1998).

Health – 60% to 90% of visits to a medical doctor may be caused or worsened by stress. Cognitive interventions may decrease the symptoms of stress (Benson, 1996).

Overcoming fear – Paratroopers who initially had high fear levels about parachuting were able to significantly decrease their fear through cognitive and physical interventions (Sapolsky, 1998).

Opportunities for Taking Advantage of Neurocognitive Plasticity

First, consider the issue of reduction in the rate of aging. Studies of people who live to be 100 years of age indicate very different cognitive strategies from those who do not. Could these strategies be learned by the rest of us? Second, consider wealth. Studies of individuals who become millionaires indicate that they have a different set of cognitive strategies than the rest of us. If these were learned, could we use this as an effective way to battle poverty?

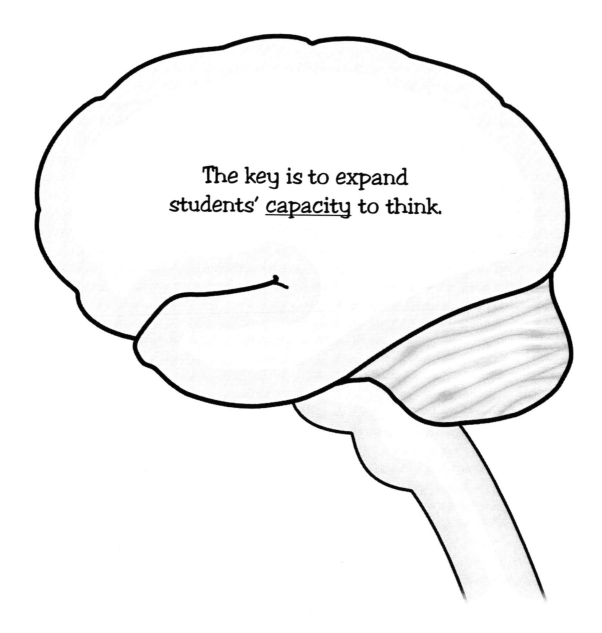

The key is to expand students' <u>capacity</u> to think.

Neurocognitive Plasticity: By What Method?

A theory without methods by which to actualize it is worth little (Deming, 1994) for it is methods that create the use of theoretical understandings. A method by which students develop the *capacity* of human beings to evidence *skills* in learning, thinking, and communicating is through coaching, or guiding, the development of specific cognitive assets.

To backtrack a bit, we support the research and practice stating that it is important that human beings have opportunity to learn in two important ways. First, it is important that children have an opportunity to explore the environment and learn through their own body-brain learning systems. This component of learning is discussed further in the BrainSMART system and is illustrated by the example of a child who explores sand in the sandbox by building castles and pouring from container to container to learn many things about sand, measurement, solids and liquids, and perhaps more. The second type of learning is guided, mediated, or coached learning and is the type of learning addressed here in the Thinking for Results system. It is through this kind of learning that the young come to know what is valued in a culture, how to behave, much about thinking, and how to live socially. This method, coaching, must be provided by a caring adult such as a parent or teacher and is the type of teaching discussed more in this text.

A System for Coaching Neurocognitive Plasticity

In workshops taught by Donna for educators from south central Los Angeles, teachers explored the concept of developing neurocognitive plasticity. Here the educators work with students who are often gang members, or at risk of engaging in gang activity. As Donna explained the input-process-output model, she asked the group, "Where do we as educators put most of our emphasis? Is it A – at the input stage, where students are gathering important sensory information; B – at the process (or elaboration) stage, when students explore and link information; or C – output, the noticeable stage where they communicate or behave in a particular way?" Of course, most of the educators chose – the output phase. They spoke of great emphasis on tests and grades!

Our experience is that the quality of student work at the output phase is almost directly proportional to how well we have cultivated the cognitive assets at the input and processing stages. As in the story of the goose that lays the golden eggs, effective school systems nurture the goose. That is, they nurture the students cognitive assets at all levels, including *input* and *processing* in order to create students who can produce great *output*.

7

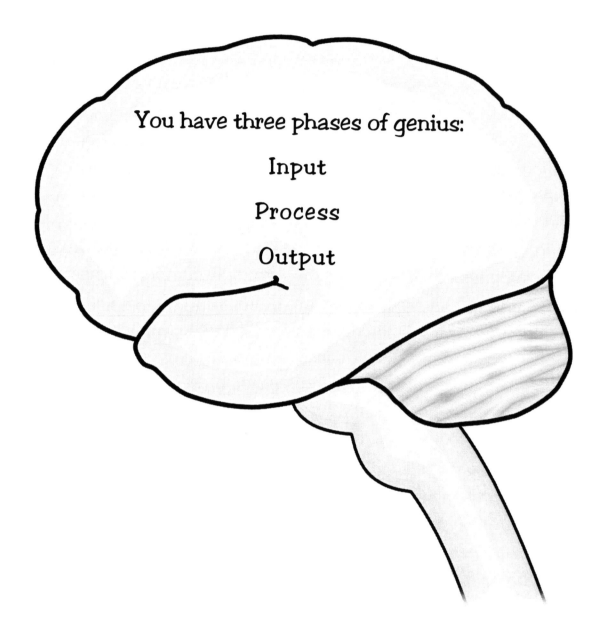

You have three phases of genius:

Input

Process

Output

The authors use the three-phase thinking model as a useful diagnostic tool in their own everyday behaviors. For example, in order to sustain the high energy level and focus necessary to create this program (our golden egg), it is essential to plan and execute regular exercise and eat nutritiously. The three-phase model is introduced and will be elaborated on later.

The Cognitive Assets In Three Phases

Input – Gather Sensory Information

- Clear intention
- Practical optimism
- Initiative
- Systematic search
- Using two or more sources of information
- Selective Attention
- Making Comparisons
- Understanding time
- Understanding space

Process – Elaboration of Thought

- Problem definition
- Classification
- Making connections
- Systematic planning
- Cognitive flexibility
- Using cues appropriately
- Making inferences/hypothetical thinking
- Working memory
- Making meaning
- Summarizing

Output – Application in the World

- Point of view
- Thoughtful behavior
- Effective expression
- Appropriate courage
- Finishing power
- Learning from experience

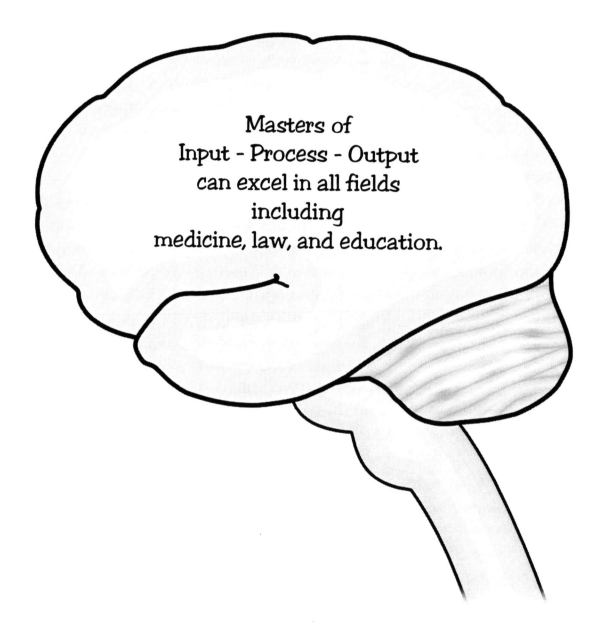

Masters of
Input - Process - Output
can excel in all fields
including
medicine, law, and education.

The Three Phases of Learning Applied to Three Careers

In our work with leaders in the fields of business, education, and health services, it has become clear that high cognitive skill in the input, process, and output areas is essential for career success. It is also clear that those students who come from economically disadvantaged communities can truly level the playing field by acquiring the cognitive assets that will propel them to success in any field. Notice the examples below:

Profession	Input	Process	Output
Doctor	diagnose symptoms	assess options	prescribe treatment
Lawyer	get case details	research prior cases	present case
Teacher	learn about subject and students	make it real	teach so students learn

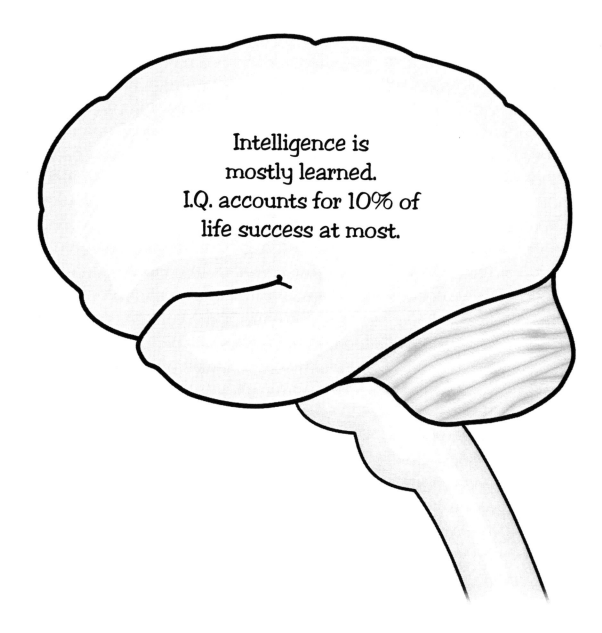

Intelligence is
mostly learned.
I.Q. accounts for 10% of
life success at most.

Chapter 2

Viewing Intelligence Differently: Helping Students Reach Their Potential!

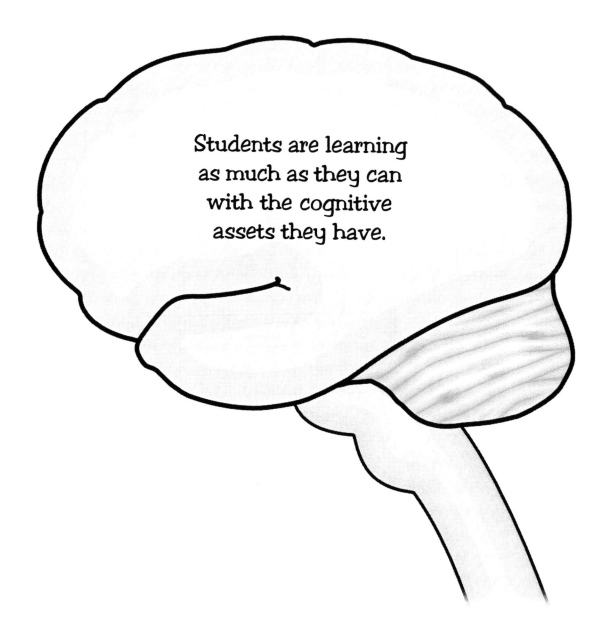

Students are learning
as much as they can
with the cognitive
assets they have.

Introduction

In this segment on human intelligence, we will start by highlighting three understandings that we believe often *limit* the way we view learning in schools and in training situations. Then we briefly highlight important work within the psychometric movement. Lastly, we introduce potential intelligence and dynamic assessment, which we believe to be very important as we seek to develop brain-compatible and thinking classrooms.

Three Common Understandings of Intelligence and Learning

It seems critical for us to amplify some understandings about learning and human intelligence that have contributed to the fact that many educators and teachers feel powerless to teach very important tools that they want their students to have and use at school! The first of three understandings about intelligence that we believe often have a negative influence in schools is the notion that psychometrics has set forth the precise measuring of static IQ and schools behaving as if it is indeed frozen and unchanging *even* when positive learning experiences happen.

The second understanding is the inappropriate use of Freud's work to "write off" children in the society if they have not been privy to a relationship where learning to learn was taught at home. An example of this understanding applied is manifest in conversations that sound like this in schools and other important agencies in our communities: "Well, I'd spend more time trying to help Jane, but you know her parents. Her father may be alcoholic. They are poor, and Jane doesn't seem to try. You know kids are formed at home. There's nothing I can do."

And the third understanding is that the notions of Skinner and other behaviorists apply to all populations of students, even if the rewards that are used as reinforcements in aspects of their outside lives are dramatically different from those at school. For example, if a student is rewarded at home for quick action in emergency situations (like on the street), their reinforcement system will not be wired for long-term goals such as those required to consider report cards and course credit. That is, they will not by wired to look for the reward in these long-term goals and probably will need coaching or guidance to rewire their frontal lobes for to reach for long-term commitments and goals! Great teachers we know take children and youth such as this child and make it a top priority to teach them the cognitive assets of impulse control and goal setting. In the minds of these teachers, the teaching of these cognitive assets is a prerequisite to the mastery of content knowledge.

15

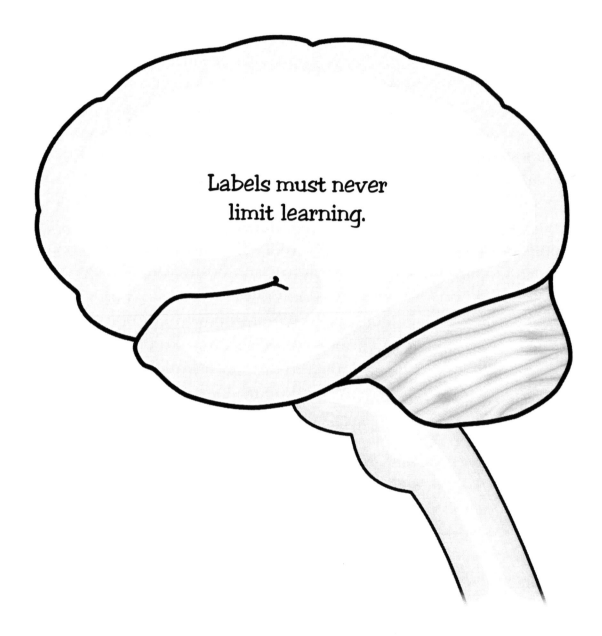

Labels must never
limit learning.

The fact of the matter is that ideas from psychometrics, behaviorism, and psychoanalysis have helped us better understand how humans learn (Dembo, 1991). For example, it is critical that as a society we understand the powerful role of parents and early childhood education in children's lives. Freud helped us understand this. However, we believe that these understandings have often been used in *systems* to limit the brains of educators and students across the life span, rather than to help expand learning opportunities for all learners, as all educators wish for and hope to do!

This is a good time to stop and reflect upon how each of these three views of intelligence has impacted schools and our society. Of course books are written on each of these three areas. What follows here are extremely brief notes.

- Psychometrics – In schools psychometrics are often used to gather numerical information about students IQ Sometimes helpful information is also explored about students' processing of information and cognitive functioning. Following the passage of PL 94-142, these understandings are used to place students in special education. The original plan was to place students, teach them to compensate, and then guide them to move out to the meaningful world of work and relationships.

- Freud's psychoanalytic breakthroughs in the early 1900s – These understandings placed a premium on early relationships and helped educators grasp the importance of the good nurturing caregiver.

- Behaviorism – These understandings place a great importance on *external* rewards and punishments. Although we believe this is important, the brain-based and cognitive movements place a premium on the development of the human brain and thinking systems *within*. (This is *not* to say that establishing rules, reward systems, and consequences are not important.)

Psychometric Understandings

All teachers want to teach students and help them reach their potential in school and life. Many of us have experienced the joy of reaching and teaching a student when someone said, "Oh, he or she can't learn that, their IQ is too low!" The fact is that today researchers say that only 4% to 10% of success is defined by intelligence (Sternberg, 1997). This new understanding explains the stories of students you might know who are classified "gifted" and still have many problems that keep success out of reach. One of the difficulties that we have seen working with the gifted population is disorganization, as if they have received so much input they don't have a way of organizing it for meaningful

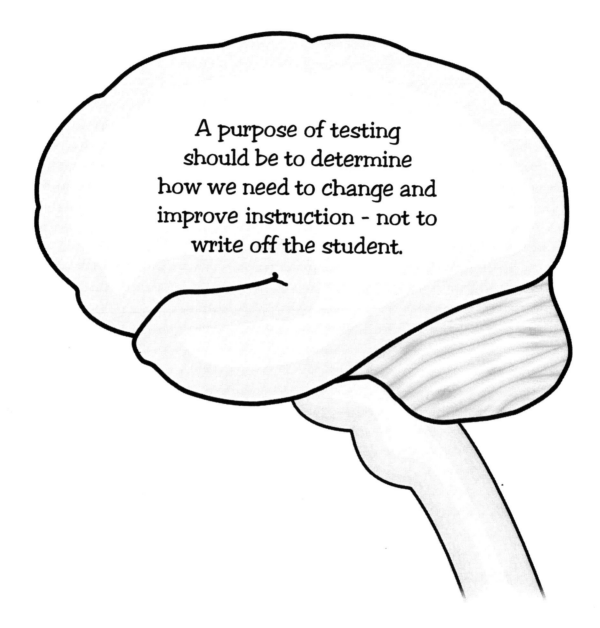

A purpose of testing should be to determine how we need to change and improve instruction - not to write off the student.

output. Or, the beautiful story of a teacher reaching a student who someone had labeled "low IQ, or gray area child." Maybe he has habits associated with optimism and hard work. Or, perhaps he learns from failure and so enjoys success!

It is from the field of psychometrics that many current understandings of intelligence have emerged over the past decades. It is psychometric measurement that yields IQ scores used to place students in special education and often in gifted programs as well. This type of assessment can also yield valuable information about students' thinking processes. However, we believe that exact measurement such as these also have been used in systems to limit many students' options in life. This type of assessment is called static IQ testing.

From an historical perspective, in 1927, Spearman proposed the general theory of intelligence. He believed that one general factor defined a person's intelligence and that if a student had difficulty in one area, so they would in another! Think of the vast difference in Spearman's theory of general intelligence and Howard Gardner's helpful, current, and brain-compatible theory of multiple intelligences.

At around the same time, Thorndike identified intelligence as having three primary abilities: abstract (ideas and symbols), mechanical (sensory-motor, or hands-on), and social. According to this model, a student could have high ability in one area and difficulty in another. You might be thinking, for example, of the professor who, lost in ideas, has difficulty tying his shoe!

Guilford, in 1959, proposed an elaborate multifactor theory of intelligence. In the Structure of Intellect (SOI) model, he defined contents, operations, and products as dimensions of human intelligence. This three-dimensional model also implies that human intelligence cannot be defined by a single score.

Potential Intelligence and Dynamic Assessment

Today, a growing number of psychologists and teachers use *dynamic,* rather than static, assessment measures to explore intelligence (Lidz, 1991). These cognitive assessment measures explore aspects of thinking or prerequisites for thinking, such as organization, understanding of space and time, and classification, to name a few. Rather than determining which number(s) best describe a student's functioning, in potential assessment we assess how much coaching the student needs to be able to master each aspect of thinking to enjoy success at school. In this type of assessment the test-teach-test method is used to begin the teaching intervention during testing.

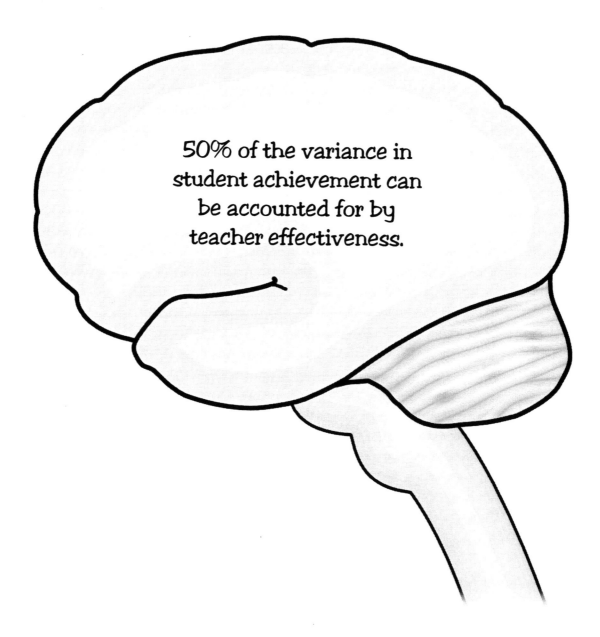

50% of the variance in student achievement can be accounted for by teacher effectiveness.

Educational psychologists, such as Donna, believe that this is often a very good assessment to use with some students. For example, it works well with students who have not had an opportunity to develop an understanding of the content in static assessments. An example of such content knowledge is "Approximately how many miles is it from New York to Los Angeles?" Many teachers and psychologists are concerned that by testing this type of knowledge, students who have not already been taught the information run a risk of being labeled and put into special classes, when, in fact, what they need is to have access to the information. Dynamic assessment also might be preferred for students with low motivation or those who have language difficulties and/or emotional problems.

The dynamic assessments are also known as authentic in that they examine the potential of students and the amount of guidance (or coaching) it will take for them to succeed in real-life tasks that require thinking. Potential intelligence is not a brand new idea. It has been described and developed by psychologist Reuven Feuerstein and his followers (Feuerstein, Feuerstein, & Gross, 1997) since the early 1950s when he accepted the charge to prepare adolescents and young adults for a life of productive work after Holocaust survival. Many had lost their families and some had difficulties such as Down's Syndrome. So, for both those who had neurobiological disorders and those who had endured great suffering in their environment, Feuerstein found out how much "teaching" they needed to be able to live out their lives successfully through assessing intellectual *potential,* not what they had already learned, or intellect they were using at that moment. He also used the information gathered to learn what cognitive skills were needed to increase performance.

Since then, this understanding of potential has been used at sites around the world, particularly where cognitive interventions are used to help students "learn to learn" so they can function "smarter." This powerful understanding has been used with students in regular education in all different subject content areas, in special education, and in gifted education across the world in order to help them learn how to learn and think in ways that have made their brains "learn smarter and do school better." In BrainSMART *Thinking for Results*, we rely on understandings that are grounded in the idea of humans reaching potential with specific methods that develop cognitive assets that are used every day of life!

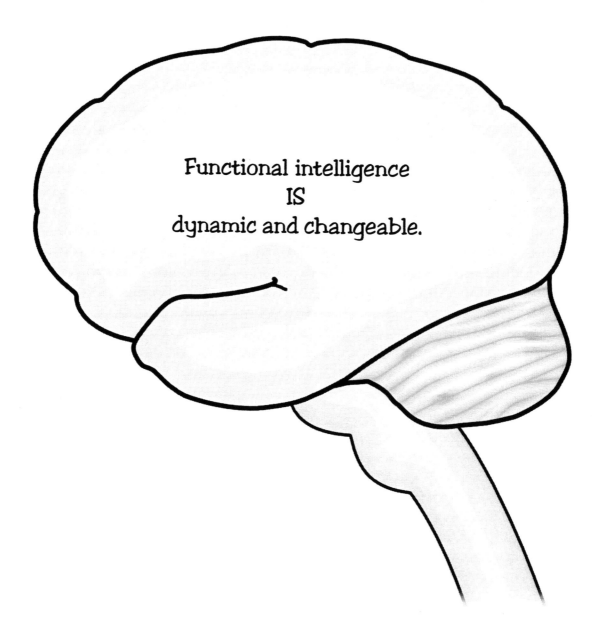

Functional intelligence
IS
dynamic and changeable.

Summary

Research suggests that a series of highly effective teachers can greatly increase student achievement regardless of the student's socioeconomic status, or other aspects of our students' lives (Duttweiler & Robinson, 1999). In fact, some 50% of the variance in student achievement can be accounted for by teacher effectiveness. The critical component here is that effective teachers believe that intelligence is not static (or fixed) and that the students who arrive in school with the least learning experiences are the ones that will benefit most from effective instruction.

What these highly effective teachers have discovered is that intelligence is, in fact, dynamic and changeable. Now cognitive neuroscience (through understandings about potential intelligence and dynamic assessment) supports this belief.

If we consider current student performance as being the indicator of what cognitive assets are currently in place, it is logical to ask "How can we cultivate a higher level of functional intelligence?" Howard Gardner once said, "It is not how smart am I, but how am I smart." We now say, "It is not just how am I smart, but how do I become smarter?"

For example, consider the cognitive asset of practical optimism, which is a critical part of emotional intelligence. Research suggests that emotional intelligence is at least as good a predictor of lifelong success as IQ. Twenty years of research by Dr. Martin Seligman (1998) demonstrates consistently that optimism can be learned. We, therefore, believe that emotional intelligence can be improved.

Again and again we have seen other cognitive assets, such as systematic planning and understanding time, improve when students learn the explicit language and concepts of thinking. As great teachers create the learning laboratory where students use the cognitive assets in academics, in social, and in life situations, they begin to learn the importance of the assets! In *Thinking for Results* we explore the methods, process, and strategies for guiding students to develop these important assets.

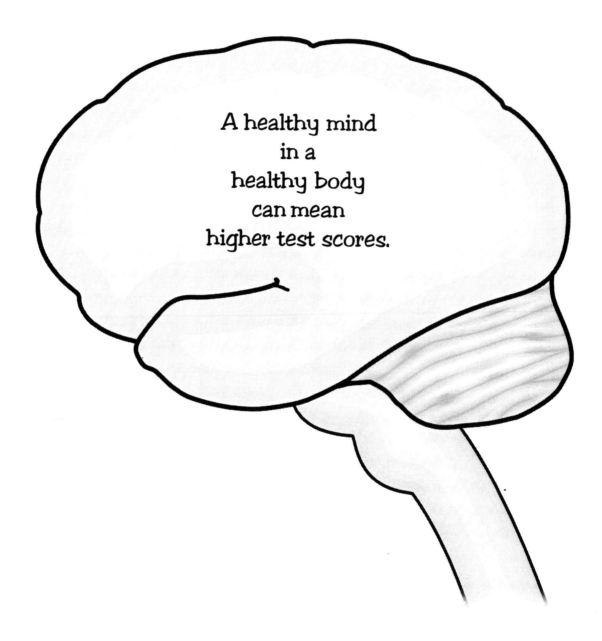

A healthy mind
in a
healthy body
can mean
higher test scores.

Chapter 3

Fitness in the BrainSMART Lab

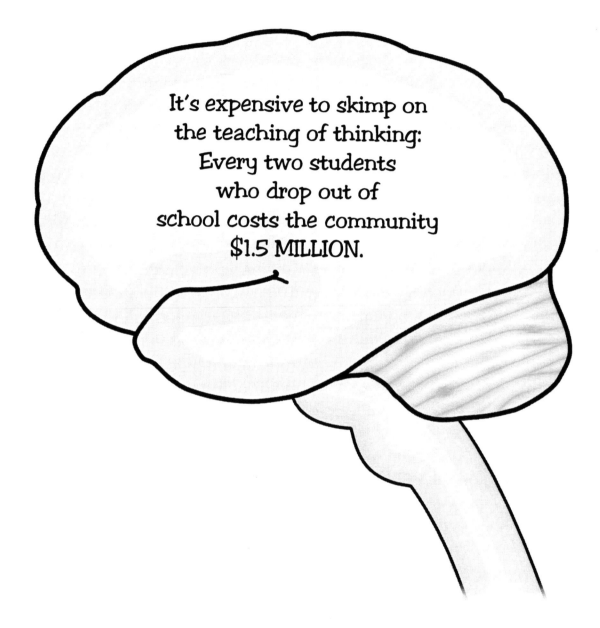

It's expensive to skimp on
the teaching of thinking:
Every two students
who drop out of
school costs the community
$1.5 MILLION.

Introduction

Research suggests that human beings think, learn and communicate most effectively when the body brain system is operating at a peak level. The interconnectedness between the brain and the central nervous system with the rest of the human physiology means that many factors influence how well we think. These factors include...

- Mood
- Exercise and movement
- Hydration level
- Nutrition
- Sleep
- Stress

Mood

Studies suggest that when people are in a positive mood they can think more creatively, find novel solutions to difficult problems, and they can sustain the optimism they need to follow through on important tasks. When people are in a negative mood however, they can find it more difficult to think creatively and they may be pessimistic about their chances of success. This can lead to low motivation to keep thinking through complex problems and lower levels of achievement.

Research suggests that people have a set point of happiness. However, by working on cognitive strategies that allow them to develop their strengths they can come to experience more joy. The importance of having a happier disposition can be profound. Several studies suggest that happier people live longer and suffer less illness. A study of the nuns of Notre Dame found that those who were identified as viewing their lives in the most positive light lived some 6.9 years longer than those who were the most negative about their lives. A long term Harvard study found that individuals with mature defenses, which includes being able to make "lemons into lemonade" had a greater chance of staying healthy than those without this mindset.

Exercise and Movement

Plato, from ancient Greece, has long been recognized as a leader in thinking. He, too, believed in the power of movement. In fact, many of his lessons were given to his students while walking in the olive groves. *Plato* was a nickname from the Greek (for *wide*) as he was a strong man and a skilled wrestler. There is much research to suggest that movement can increase student achievement and reduce stress.

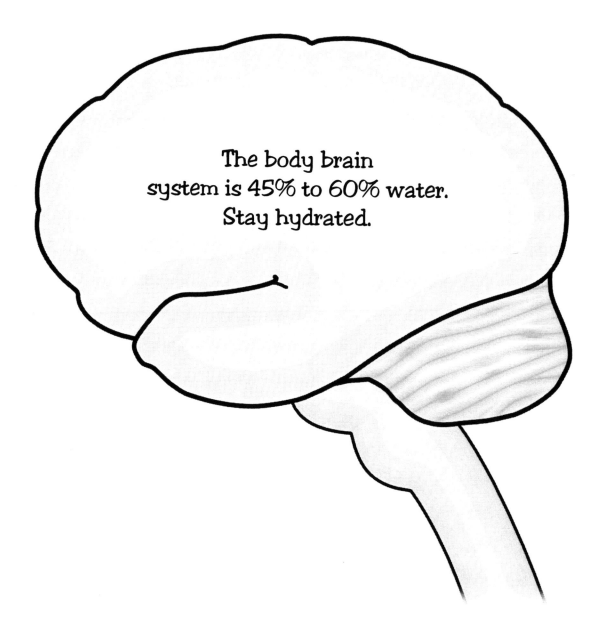

The body brain system is 45% to 60% water. Stay hydrated.

Research suggests that movement is essential in order for the body brain system to be in a peak state for thinking and learning (Ratey, 2001). For example, Harvard researcher, Dr. John Ratey, highlights the beneficial impact of martial arts for individuals with attention deficit disorder. Furthermore, the act of standing or walking can increase the blood supply to the thinking areas of the brain quite significantly. Breakthroughs in cognitive neuroscience indicate that various movements require extremely high levels of cognitive function.

Hydration Level

Around 45% to 60% of your body weight is water. That is around nine gallons for the average woman. On an average day, your brain-body system uses at least four cups of your water supply for metabolic processes, removing wastes, and regulating temperature. The best guide for your need to consume more water is thirst. Many experts recommend that you drink about eight glasses of water a day.

It is critical to sustain a good level of hydration for your brain-body system to function at peak levels. Your brain is an electrical and chemical system that requires adequate levels of water for effective transmission of information.

Nutrition

Research at MIT sponsored by the United States military (Wurtman, 1986) suggests a practical eating plan for maximum energy and focus for you and your family, and we strongly suggest it for school meals and snacks as well. It is suggested that when you eat a high carbohydrate meal, such as pasta, sandwiches, or sugary snacks, you can create a sugar crash in your brain.

As you eat more carbohydrates than you need, your blood sugar level may shoot up, giving you a short-term sugar high. Then, the hormone insulin is released from the pancreas to get excess sugar levels out of your blood stream. The insulin is so efficient at moving sugar into your fat cells that it increases the flow of glucose to your brain. Therefore, you may feel drowsy and find it difficult to concentrate on important tasks. If you want to be sharp, smart, and energized, research suggests that you should start your meal with protein, such as fish, meat, or nuts. The protein stimulates release of the hormone glucagon. This wonderful chemical instructs your fat cells to release their stored energy to give your brain a smooth flow of fuel for peak levels of attention. Other chemicals that are released as a result of protein consumption are tyrosine and, subsequently, dopamine which drives good feeling and sharp attention in the neurocognitive system.

If the body doesn't move,
the brain may not learn at optimum levels.

So what does this mean when it comes to feeding your family or for school meals that fuel laser-sharp attention? <u>Breakfast</u>, we should get a good hit of protein. For example, a quick egg-white omelet with a bit of low fat cheese, or some peanuts will get the job done. Or, oatmeal, which provides good slow release carbohydrates and high fiber content for radiant health. <u>Lunchtime</u>, school lunchrooms should be full of fruits, milk, and low fat protein, such as chicken, together with salad or chopped vegetables. <u>Supper</u>, you can consume more comfort carbohydrates such as pasta or fresh potatoes, along with fish, meat, or vegetarian delights that you most enjoy! The potatoes or pasta will help to trigger the release of tryptophan and, subsequently, the feel-calm-and-blissful neurotransmitter serotonin.

Remember that food is the pharmacy of feeling good, staying focused and energized, or relaxed and calm. The bottom line is that how you eat, think, and exercise may have as powerful an impact on your brain as most doctor-prescribed drugs. (However, it is important that we continue to consult a physician to obtain checkups and treatment when necessary.)

Sleep

Most Americans are sleep deprived. This has a significant impact on cognitive processes. Therefore it is suggested that most adults require a minimum of at least 7.5 hours of sleep per night. It is essential that children get sufficient sleep. In the teen years many students do not fire up their brains for high levels of learning until mid-morning. It would be beneficial to start school later, or to ensure that the most critical information is studied any time other than the first couple of hours of the day.

Sleep is an integral and critical part of the brain-body system's learning process. For example, have you ever studied something during the day and not quite understood it, then awoke the next day to find it clearly understood in your mind? When you sleep, many of your conscious processes are taken "off line," which allows your wonderful unconscious processes to sort and store the learning experiences of your day. Research has discovered that when human subjects were awakened throughout the night, their recall of information studied was significantly reduced.

Stress

Current research indicates that higher order thinking is supported by the frontal brain area (Carter, 1999). When you are in what we call SMART state, you can input, process, and output well. When you are stressed, you backshift to a stressed state where you find it difficult to think well.

In the *Thinking for Results* approach, we believe that a foundational aspect

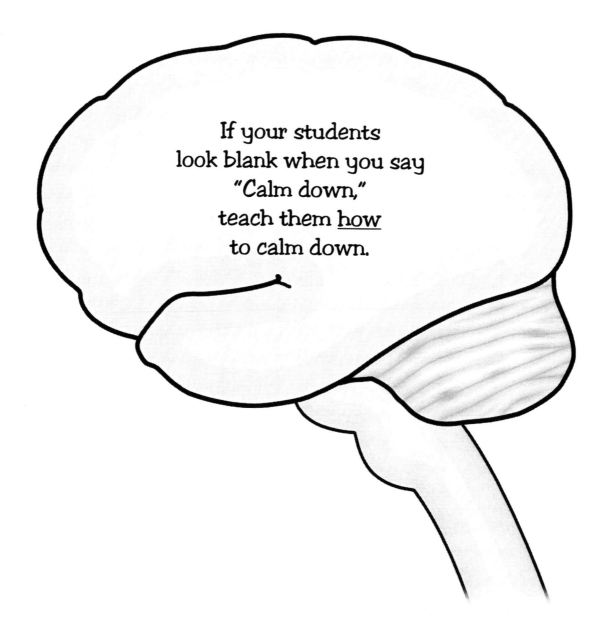

If your students
look blank when you say
"Calm down,"
teach them <u>how</u>
to calm down.

for creating classrooms of maximum thinking is that the entire body-brain system is involved in learning. So, in this chapter, we highlight some aspects of the body system that are important for learning to take place. Then, we share our BrainObics™ system for a specific kind of exercise that helps students learn.

Elsewhere in the program we amplify the importance of other components for structuring powerful learning labs. Generally the other components are: direct and coached learning, cultivating cognitive assets, learning with three modalities, learning across the school site, and parent education.

Think of a time when you felt like you were really on top of your game. You were relaxed, confident, able to concentrate, solve problems, and really enjoy the process. You were really accessing your brain's potential. Now, what would happen if you suddenly got stressed? What would happen to your ability to think clearly and act intelligently to achieve your goals? If you are like most of us, you would suddenly lose this ability. Research suggests that there is a physiological basis to this. In fact, brain scans indicate that energy moves away from the frontal area and down into lower brain systems.

Many students and staff arrive in the classroom in stressed states. It is important to move the energy to the frontal areas of the brain — to a state where you can think well. We call this frontshifting. To do this we need to manage the factors that can positively influence state and increase thinking.

BrainObics

During our BrainSMART workshops one of the most popular activities have been what we call *BrainObics*. BrainObics includes a simple system of exercises designed to optimize the body-brain system for thinking and learning. The exercises include activities where students cross the midline with cross-lateral movements, which may integrate the left and right hemispheres for better functioning.

As we visit schools across the United States, it is wonderful to see students come to life as they do these exercises to burn off surplus energy and get refreshed and refocused on their thinking and learning tasks. Refer to the appendix for a group of BrainObics exercises.

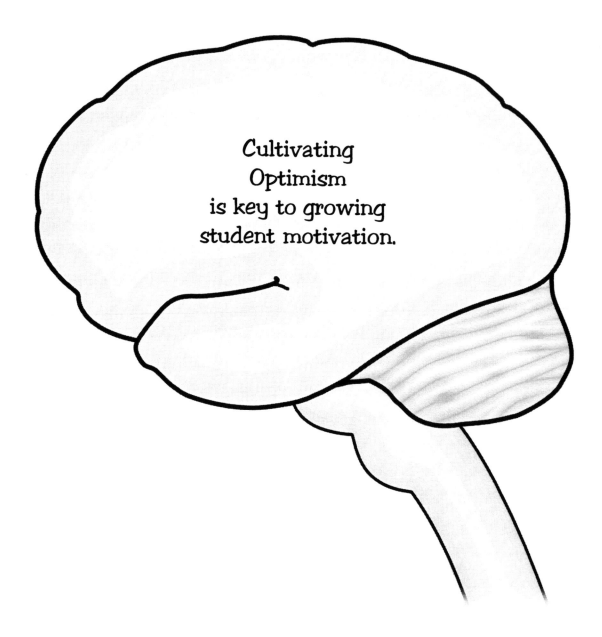

Cultivating
Optimism
is key to growing
student motivation.

Other Important Aspects of The BrainSMART Lab for Thinking

Parent Education

It is important to remember that students spend a relatively small time in the classroom in their developing years. In fact, up to age 18, students spend only 13% of their waking hours in school. The remaining 87% spent outside of school, and theoretically, are influenced by their parents. In our *BrainSMART In the House* workshops that we hold with parents and parent educators across the United States, it is wonderful to see how excited parents get at the prospect of influencing positively their children's thinking skills. It is very clear in these highly energized workshops that the parents intend to transfer what they have learned immediately to themselves and their children. For example, many parents welcome the opportunity presented by the thinking processes of practical optimism in such a way as to increase their children's optimism. Or, to teach the cognitive asset organizing space so that rooms and minds are tidier. For more information about parent education, see *BrainSMART In the House* at www.brainsmart.com.

Cultivating Cognitive Assets

In *Thinking for Results,* 25 important cognitive aspects are named and explained. In the BrainSMART lab for thinking, these cognitive assets are front and center of good instruction. They are introduced and then woven into all content area, life, and social skill examples. It is emphasized that these are keys to many successes!

Whenever possible, use graphics to illustrate these cognitive assets. Let students draw them out! Use posters. Highlight them. Students in the laboratory really enjoy using the now famous brain car for learning to drive their own brains. (See the brain car in the appendix.) Graphics help students (even the younger elementary children) begin to make meaning of the cognitive assets which tend to be quite abstract.

Learning Across the School Site

We know that individual teachers and their approaches to instruction have a huge impact on children, youth, and learning. Beyond the confines of their own classrooms these teachers can be a positive influence on the whole school. We have been blessed to visit schools where a few highly effective teachers team together to be a catalyst for building positive expectations for all students. They achieve this by their positive enthusiasm during professional development days and workshops, their willingness to help new teachers, and

35

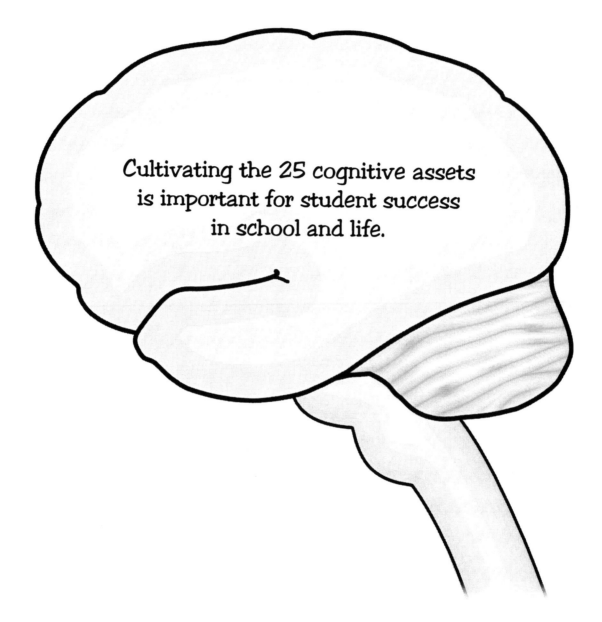

Cultivating the 25 cognitive assets
is important for student success
in school and life.

their genuine desire to share what is working for them.

On the other hand, we have also been to schools where a few teachers with negative attitudes can create a culture of cynicism and low expectations that pollutes the atmosphere for other teachers and students. The research is clear that when expectations and beliefs change, often inspired by new instructional strategies, then the culture can shift from blaming students to a focus on improving instructional effectiveness. One of our faculty and friends is very clear in her instructions about what new teachers need to do and what to avoid when they come to a school. She is adamant that they should not waste time in the teacher's lounge listening to negative talk about students.

We have been fortunate to have met true instructional leaders who strongly and positively influence school culture where everyone is thinking and learning. These leaders often work very hard at thinking aloud to mediate higher-order thinking for faculty and students. A good example of an effective instructional leader is a principal who consistently sends her teachers to workshops. One of her teachers said, "My principal never asks me to do anything I have not been trained to do." Effective classroom teachers are also very careful to support their school leaders and to ask for what they need to improve their skills so their students learn more.

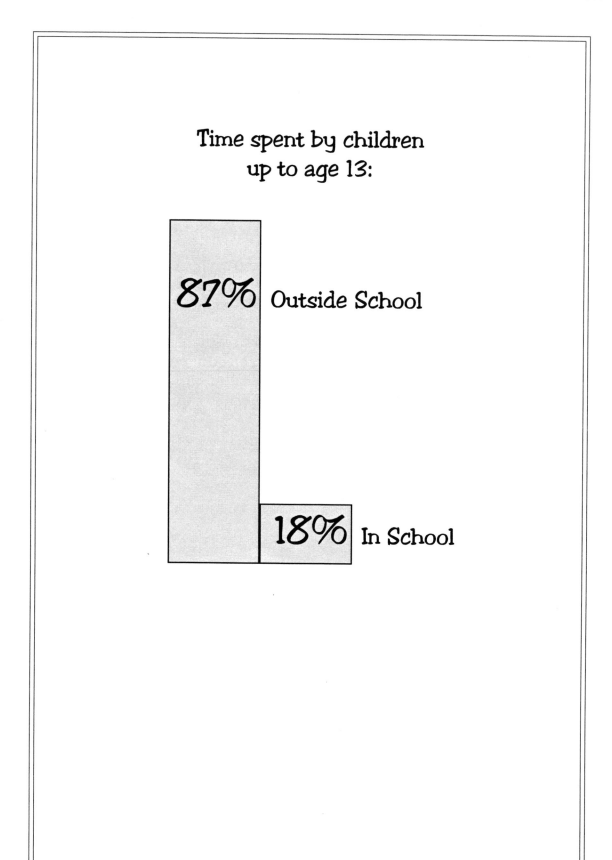

Time spent by children
up to age 13:

87% Outside School

18% In School

Chapter 4

Coaching:
The Secret of Champions

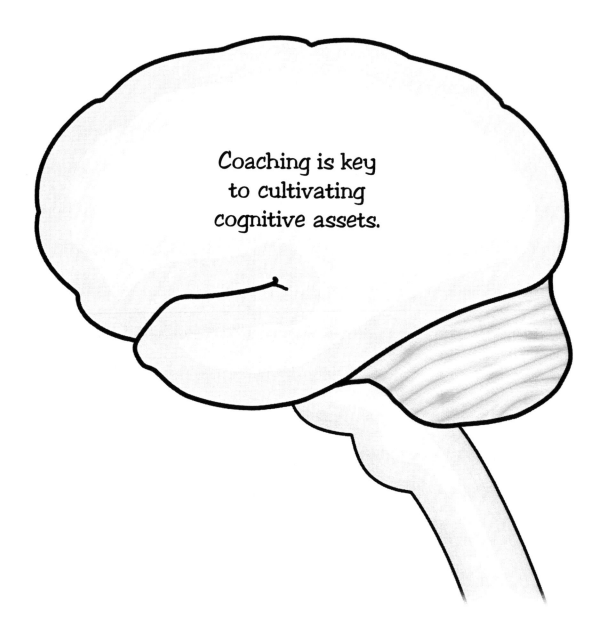

Coaching is key
to cultivating
cognitive assets.

Introduction

Research indicates that it is important for human beings to have at least one significant partnership so that they can be successful learners and thinkers (Feuerstein, Rand, Hoffman, & Miller, 1980). And, most important today, learn how to learn. The partner may be a teacher, parent, or mentor.

Generally humans learn in two basic ways that you may have observed in your life and with children. One way that we learn is directly in the environment. The environment provides the stimulus and we respond to it in some way. For example, children and youth learn many things by watching television at home, or reading a book. This is the type of learning about which Piaget spoke and wrote. Maybe you remember his accounts of Jacqueline, his daughter, and other children learning naturally.

The second way that humans learn is in partnership with a more experienced learner — an adult who can teach the less experienced other (child, youth, student) to learn how to learn. It is in these important social relationships that children learn how to think and develop the ability to be successful. The coaching aspect of learning/teaching is the topic of this chapter.

Underlying Principles of Coaching for Thinking

There are some major principles in a classroom in which the teacher is a mediational coach for learning and thinking. First, the environment is arranged for maximum interaction among teacher and students, students learning together, and students interacting with engaging materials. The classroom is an exciting laboratory for learning.

Second, the teacher as mediator/coach is a partner in relationship with the learners. Teachers are consistently engaged in their own challenging problems and are in touch with the joys and difficulties that arise when learning happens. Therefore, courageous teachers model practical optimism as they guide learners to solve problems. Additionally, often teachers who use this method help students become better thinkers by questioning, rather than lecturing students to learn individually. You probably recognize this as the technique Socrates and other great teachers have used throughout the ages. It engages students while making them aware of their process of thinking as they learn to question themselves.

Last, installing and creating habits for thinking and learning are at the very front and center of the classroom for thinking. This is important for all students; however, it is critical for at-risk learners because if they do not have an opportunity to create important thinking and learning habits, they will continue to fall behind and experience greater and greater frustration.

41

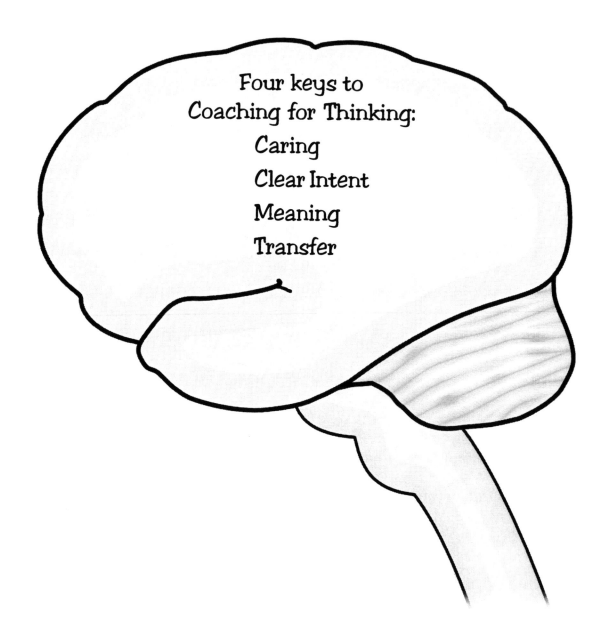

Four keys to
Coaching for Thinking:
Caring
Clear Intent
Meaning
Transfer

Four Important Keys To Coaching for Thinking

So, with these things in mind, we continue now with some of the most important keys to coaching students to learn to learn! These keys are care and concern for students as human beings; our intent to create learners who know how to learn and think; the making of meaning in our learners' minds; and the transfer of the experience of learning to other situations outside of the original one to life and academic experiences. In the big picture of our students' learning lives, we always have the intent that they are becoming more and more independent in their skill at learning! We are speaking of a specific type of transfer — transfer that extends both across life and forward into the future of ever more successful learning!

Caring

Simply put, human caring is the force that fuels coaching for thinking. It is that capacity good parents and teachers have for nurturing young. And, although caring is not enough by itself to create students who are good thinkers, it is a necessary prerequisite and not just a touchy-feely notion.

When we read Siegal's book, *The Developing Mind* (1999), we come to understand the importance of coaching for learning ideas in terms of the physical development of the human brain. The area toward the front one third of the brain and on the right side within the interior region is called the *orbital frontal cortex*. Neuroscientists believe it is within this area that the brain is actually shaped first in early life by social relationships with significant others.

Vaughan (1997), another medical doctor, speaks of the re-formation of this orbital frontal region within healing relationships, such as psychotherapy, in her book *The Talking Cure*. She also discusses the corto-limbic loop in this same region of the cortex, but extending down deep into the limbic region, as the center for the re-wiring of the brain when new understandings occur in healing relationships. For example, over time in a caring relationship, an abused woman begins to see herself as worthy of respect and care from someone. She then begins to actually rewire this in her brain as she continues to be treated with respect in the healing relationship. Next, as the brain chemicals change more and more and the rewiring continues, she actually seeks out relationships that are respectful rather than abusive. We believe that with positive and powerful relationships between teachers and mentors and the students they teach, this rewiring may be actually happening in the brain.

From a psychological perspective Feuerstein (Feuerstein, Rand, & Hoffman, 1979) coined the phrase *structural cognitive modifiability* to define what happens in the mind as humans learn how to learn. The United States National Research

43

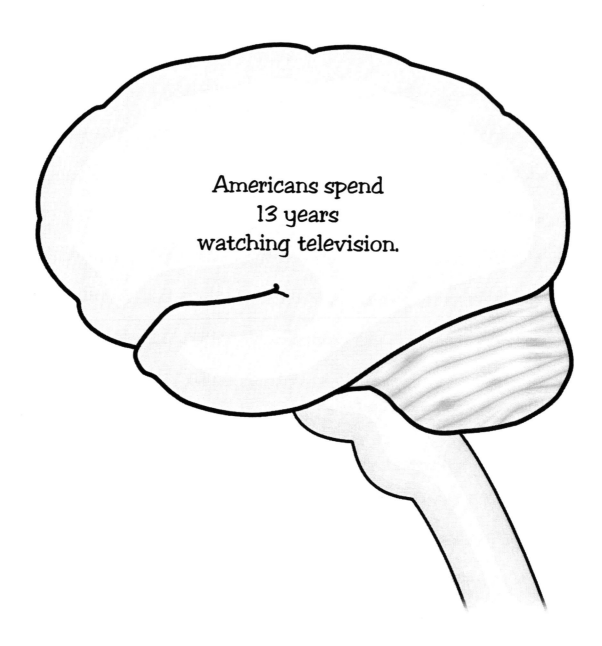

Americans spend
13 years
watching television.

Council (Branford, Brown, & Cocking, 1999) has stated that learning changes the physical structure of the human brain and that learning experiences organize and reorganize the brain in powerful ways. We think of this change in cognitive function, development of more capacity, and physical change in the brain - as neurocognitive restructuring. Or, in the short form, rewiring. This body of research clearly suggests that coaching by parents and/or teachers is very important as students learn to think independently. So, let's go forward and explore important key things to consider as we teach students to learn how to learn.

Clear Intent

Imagine yourself as a teacher holding up a magnifying glass in order to draw learners into a subject for study, to bring the contents into sharp focus! This is what we mean by *intent*. Think of the massive amount of intellectual and sensory stimulation today. This is the case due primarily to two factors. The first is that as we moved from the Industrial Age to the Information Age, we quickly increased the amount of information available to people in newspapers, on television, on computers, and elsewhere. The second fact is that stimulation for many young people today is dramatically different. It is amped up, louder, more graphic, and emotionally charged.

These factors make it very important for educators and parents to make certain that their intent is clear, and clearly important for learning. Of course, just because we have intent, doesn't mean that we will automatically have the learners' attention. So, an important part of this key factor is to invite the learner into the learning in ways that will motivate them. As educators, we are using intent only when our learners respond with a state of vigilance and attention to the learning at hand.

There are two components that learning coaches use to influence intent resulting in learner involvement. The first of these is the learning coach themselves. A few of the many ways that good learning coaches establish their intent are (a) the use of big gestures, (b) location in the room, and (c) language, including their pace and pitch. Many very effective teachers also use props and costumes to make learning happen! The other element is the stimulus, which can include effective use of all three modalities, visual and kinesthetic, as well as auditory, effective use of color, interesting questions, the use of lots of real life learning, role play, debate, and games for learning to name only a few.

To summarize the idea of clear intent, we might also imagine a hook that captures the interest of the learner and makes them want to know more about what you introduce. You — the coach — with your materials, presentation, and facilitation are the hook!

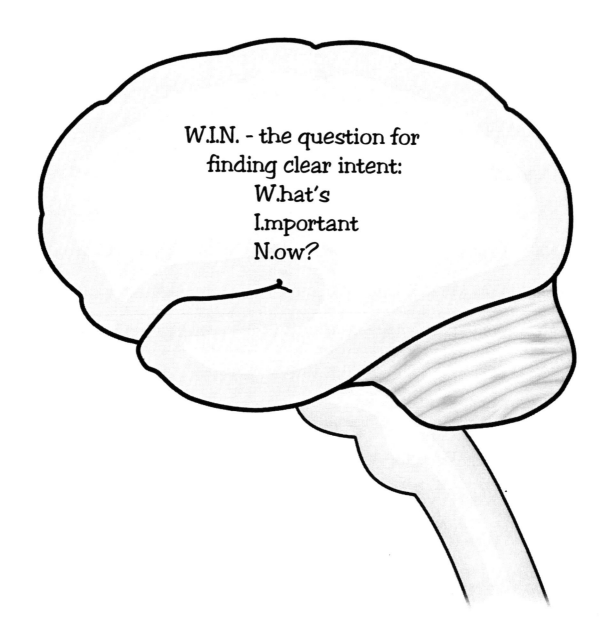

Examples of Clear Intent

An example of intent is as follows. We are currently planning a lesson on learning science and the brain with second graders. Our intent is to create a very interesting lesson that will inspire them to be curious about the brain and how they learn. The lesson will begin as I show them a brain prop and ask, "How many of you would like to know more about the brain so that you can be a better learner?"

In order to facilitate your use of clear intent, consider the following ideas:

- When considering what to teach and what your intent is in teaching it, think of the 80/20 Rule. That is, the rule that states that in life 20% of what we do gets 80% of the results. Is what you are considering teaching *in the important 20%?* That is, will it make an important positive difference in the lives of your students?

- If you do not know what you intend for the students to learn and how it can enrich their learning lives, perhaps this particular lesson is not worthy of your time, or your students' time. Remember Costa's idea of curriculum abandonment and do it! Good teachers believe that there are many important things they need to teach and no time to waste on less important ideas and action!

- Before teaching ritual
  Ask yourself - What intention am I absolutely committed to as I teach this lesson?

- During teaching ritual
  Ask yourself - How is my teaching aligning with my intentionality?

- After teaching ritual reflection
  Ask yourself - Did this lesson capture my students' attention?
  If yes, celebrate success! If not, ask what can I do differently the next time?

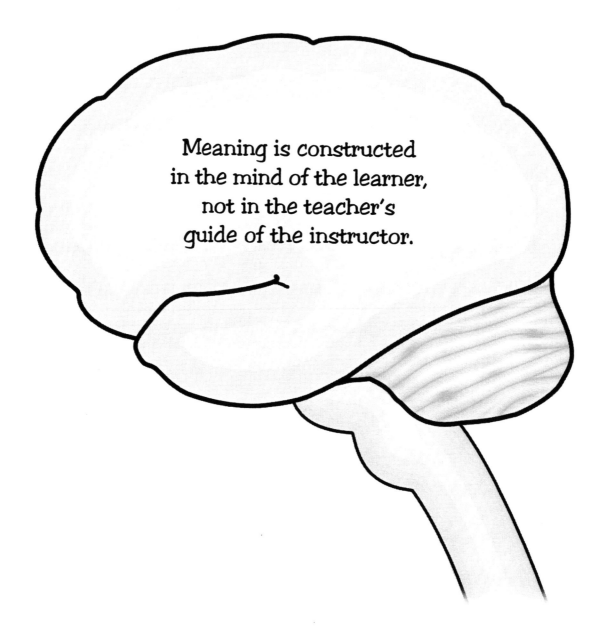

Meaning is constructed
in the mind of the learner,
not in the teacher's
guide of the instructor.

Meaning

Both meaning and transfer, the third and fourth keys to effective coaching for thinking, are covered in other BrainSMART programs. Here we amplify some important aspects of both in terms of the *Thinking for Results* program.

One important aspect of meaning is that it is obtained within a culture. For example, think of that which gives your own life meaning. You might recall how a more experienced other, perhaps a parent, mentor, or teacher, introduced you to something with care and energy and then you began to enjoy it as they did! I (Donna) think back to the way reading was such a positive time for me with my mother. I would pick out my favorite book, snuggle on her lap, and I showed off my reading to her as she enjoyed her daughter. Another example, I learned to love travel as I listened intently to my aunts' stories of travel to exciting places far away from the small town where I grew up. Then later, I wanted to teach so that I could transform lives the way special teachers guided me to transform mine.

If my mother had not have given special meaning to reading, I would have been relied more upon my teachers to infuse reading with meaning. Through their energy and influence upon me, my teachers were catalysts for my becoming a better teacher and going back to graduate school. Each of you has had the experience of being that teacher who is the bridge or coach — so very necessary to many young today so that they make meaning at school. That is, they become excited about learning, thinking, reading, writing, and math because you help them make meaning from school experiences.

Last and of critical importance to this program is the understanding of cognitive schema and meaning. For our students to be able to make meaning at school, they must be able to access something in their memory to build the meaning upon. Throughout *Thinking for Results* classroom scenes, you will notice that we are always concerned with the students' answers to our questions. We pose many questions in the course of the lesson. The questions are designed to engage the students in meaningful thinking about the lesson. And, they also help us understand what their cognitive schemas are made of. Often we use graphics, metaphors, and comparisons as well, specifically so that some abstract concepts that are difficult to understand make meaning.

Transfer

Now, think for a moment and reflect upon that student who cannot usually remember what he did in the 1 o'clock class that he is in before attending yours at 2 o'clock. Or, the time that you remembered information right up until you took the important test! Transfer, the fourth key element for effective coaching, …indeed is critically important. In the *Teaching for Results* program, notice that

49

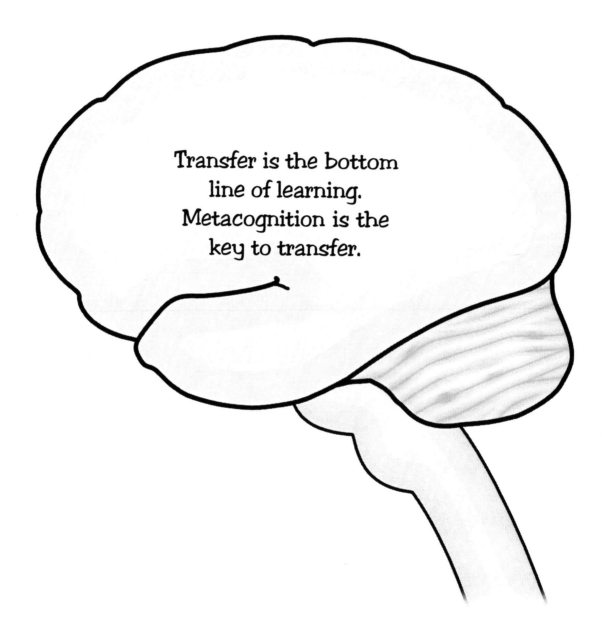

Transfer is the bottom
line of learning.
Metacognition is the
key to transfer.

we use very *explicit* language for transfer. In the classroom video footage, notice that we often ask the students to generate *their own* examples illustrating three general situations when the particular thinking skill might be used. The three situations are at school in academics, in life or in a social situation, and when older students or young children's parents might use it at work.

Take for example, the cognitive asset, understanding time. We believe that as we help students understand time as critical to their success, it is important that they have an opportunity to generate examples relevant to their lives. Often they will speak of having points subtracted for tardiness in arriving at school or handing in late papers, punishment for not making it home on time after play, and the importance of parents' being on time to work. We refer to this element of teaching as *bridging*. By this we mean taking the important cognitive asset, or element of thinking, into important areas where students need to use them in order to succeed. This practice is a part of the habits we develop in our classrooms as labs for learning.

Implementation Hints for Coaching

As you further think about coaching your students to be more effective at thinking consider the following as important keys to implementation:

1. Reflecting upon one's own application of cognitive assets. In order to coach and cultivate cognitive assets, it is important to be aware of how we use them ourselves. For example, a coach who is keen to teach the asset of clear intent could really focus on how well they use that asset in their everyday lives. In the classroom, are they clear about what their intent is in terms of facilitating student learning? In their relationships, are they clear about what and how they want to communicate? Having reflected on this and rehearsed ways to improve this asset, they are then ready to coach it with their students.

2. Setting a standard for cognitive performance. Research suggests that it is critically important to have a clear and specific standard for student achievement. In *Thinking for Results* we have developed the *Thinking for Results* Assessment to help measure current cognitive performance against a clear benchmark. (See the assessment in the appendix.)

3. Projecting belief that students can become independent thinkers and successful learners. It is well supported by many research studies that teacher expectations are a major influence on student motivation and achievement. We believe that when it comes to coaching for

51

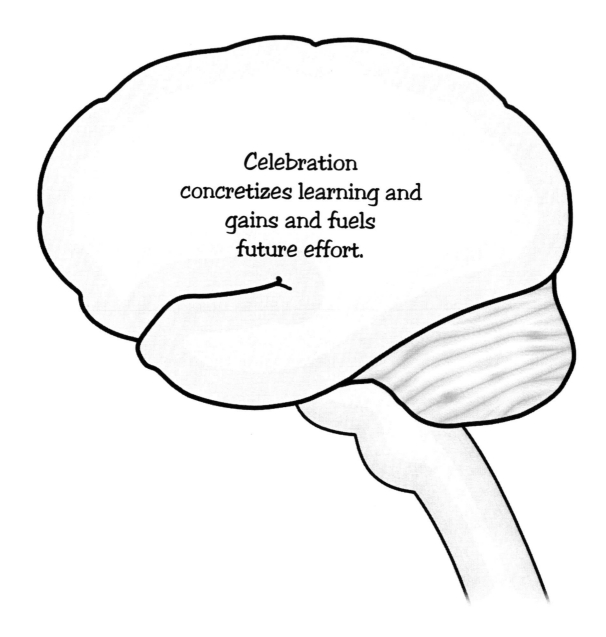

Celebration
concretizes learning and
gains and fuels
future effort.

thinking, this is particularly true. A good coach will clearly project and demonstrate through thought, word, and action that students will cultivate the cognitive assets that they need to be successful. This type of coach also experiences themselves as a partner with the student in the thinking process. That is, they consider themselves a partner who installs the cognitive assets into the students' schema.

4. Asking guiding questions instead of telling. Research in thinking and reading shows that it is very important to ask questions to create a thinking environment. Good questions help students link the new content to their existing schema and create the setting for involvement, rather than exhibit passivity.

5. Celebrating brain gains! Effective coaches work hard at helping students celebrate the improvements they make in applying their cognitive assets. This is the fuel of almost exponential improvement. For example, a coach might say "That's great use of the summarizing asset. In the past you were not as clear or brief. This time you were clear, brief, and still mentioned the four key points of the issue. Bravo! Once you have made this kind of summary, you can do it every time!" This is very important when a student who used to ramble on and on speaks clearly and succinctly and articulates all key points.

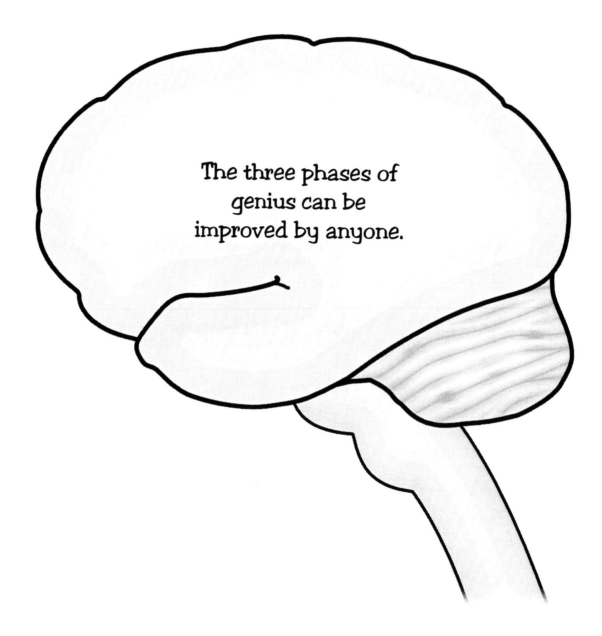

The three phases of genius can be improved by anyone.

Chapter 5
Three Phases of Genius

Metacognition may be the most important student characteristic for high student achievement.

Introduction

The explosion in research on the brain and cognitive processing offers exciting opportunities for helping educators understand the mysteries of thought. During the 21st century, the ability to think effectively may be as important as the ability to read and write. For example, what is the point of being able to decode words at high speed from a page without the skill of understanding, reflecting upon, and applying what has been read? Furthermore, the research is clear that, in order to write well, one must first learn to think well.

At BrainSMART, cognitive assets are what we call necessary skills that humans need to be able to exhibit appropriate behavior and earn high marks at school. The most exciting aspect of this work is that these cognitive assets are teachable! One way to help us deepen our understanding of these assets is to understand them as a three-part model of the thinking process. Our life's work strongly supports the belief that when we cultivate a system of skills that are necessary for success, we are truly giving students what they need for school and life.

Having established the overarching benefits of learning to think more effectively, we now focus on the three phases and specific cognitive assets that make up the process. The first phase of the information processing model that we use is called *input*. It is so called because the skills learned in this phase are necessary cognitive assets for the gathering of sensory information that can lead to a successful outcome. The second phase of the model is called *processing*. In this phase, after the information is gathered in *input*, the brain continues to elaborate upon, or process, the information that it has gathered. The last phase is the *output* phase, which we call output or communication. It is in this phase the rewards of a job well done in input and processing are seen. It is also this phase problems are seen that actually originate in either *input* or *processing*.

The three phases of genius and cognitive assets are interconnected. When our students make responses that are successful, we do not need to be so concerned with an analysis of their answers or performance. However, when there is difficulty, it becomes important to break down the response into the three-phase model complete with cognitive assets. To illustrate this point, consider the student who has difficulty because of imprecise gathering of information at the input phase. This student may have the skills in place at the output level and generally may process effectively, but may be somewhat impulsive and quick to consider the necessary information. Or, a group of students may have an unsuccessful outcome due to difficulty with the output phase after the successful gathering and processing of the information. Or,

Metacognition is key to increasing student achievement.

occasionally students will be able to successfully gather needed sensory information and prepare output effectively, but will still need coaching on some of the cognitive assets within the processing phase.

In order to cultivate the assets that students need for success in school and in life, each child must have an effective learning coach. In our model, the coach is the guide that leads students to be metacognitive and to discover the power of being the boss of their own brains. The coach also needs to teach students specifically the three phases of genius model that includes the 25 cognitive assets necessary for success.

Metacognition

Research suggests that one key to becoming happy and sustaining happiness over the long term is the ability to feel in control of one's life. On the other hand, many individuals who feel powerless to control their lives suffer stress and a loss of joy and happiness. The key pathway to achieving a positive sense of control is to understand that human beings have the power to become aware of their thoughts and to change them when necessary. This ability of thinking about one's thinking and changing it when necessary may be described as metacognition.

In a very important meta-analysis of predictors of high student achievement, researchers at the University of Chicago (Wang, Haertel, & Walberg, 1993) have reported that the *most* important student characteristic for high student achievement is metacognition. The good news is, as with other aspects of thinking, metacognition is teachable and learnable.

Additionally, this study revealed that two related criteria are extremely important for developing high student achievers. In addition to being metacognitive (thinking about their thinking), the study emphasized (a) that it is important for students to learn to think through a caring relationship with their teacher, and (b) that it is necessary to teach students to use specific aspects of thinking effectively.

Make It Practical—Drive Your Brain

In our workshops with K-12 students, we use the metaphor of "Driving Your Brain" as a concrete way to describe metacognition. Students readily grasp this concept and immediately see its value. This metaphor also taps into their innate desire to master the skills for driving their destiny, that is, to learn to be the boss of their own brains. For example, students can recognize times when they needed to put the brakes on their brains in order to avoid behaviors that could have led to problems. They also can see the need to keep their brain moving in the right lane and in the right direction toward their goals. In fact, a

59

Every day at school, students
are expected to use the cognitive assets.
Therefore, isn't it important
to teach them every day?

great exercise that teachers often do is to get students to brainstorm the benefits of driving their brains in school and in life.

Key Aspects of Cognitive Assets

First, they are *not* either there or not as a part of personality. They *are* teachable.

Second, cognitive assets are developed within culture. For example, the asset of time is learned with others in family and community. If a child is from a culture that understands time in large blocks, not in discrete units, they might often be disciplined at school for being late. Students must be on time at school because many people are organized to be at certain places at certain times of the day. This is very different from many of our students' culture at home, where time is seen in much larger units and being minutes late is not punished. Therefore, with the asset of time as well as others, it is important for parents to have the opportunity to learn about the cognitive assets necessary for school so that they can reinforce them at home.

Third, the presence or absence of cognitive assets, to a great extent, determines the behavior, grades, and life successes of human beings. We believe that the cognitive assets are part of the 20% of what we do that gets 80% of the results. They are very important.

Fourth, if students do not have the cognitive assets they are at great risk at school.

Fifth, students who have special neurobiological issues, such as Down's Syndrome, or other difficulties, need to learn the cognitive assets too. Also, students who have attention problems and associated difficulty with lethargy and/or hyperactivity benefit greatly from learning the cognitive assets.

Sixth, although our schools fully expect students to use cognitive assets to manage their learning and behavior, they do not usually teach students these assets. Many students have difficulty at school and cause teachers to be concerned because they simply have not developed the thinking tools they need. When the tools are taught explicitly, and students learn them, it makes a world of difference in their behavior, achievement, and life.

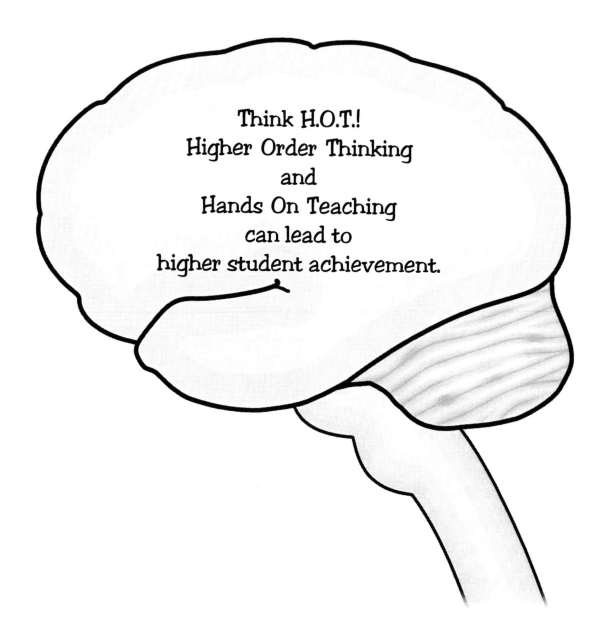

Think H.O.T.!
Higher Order Thinking
and
Hands On Teaching
can lead to
higher student achievement.

Twenty-Five Cognitive Assets Within Three Phases and Their Definition

Input – Gathering Sensory Information

- Clear Intent – Sustaining a clear sense of what one's intentions are in each situation. For example, the teacher who has the clear intention of increasing student learning by constantly improving their instructional skills will tend to increase their effectiveness and achieve their goals.

- Practical Optimism – An approach to life that focuses on taking practical positive action to increase the probability of successful outcomes.

- Initiative – Readiness and skill in taking action.

- Systematic Search –Appropriate exploratory behavior that is organized in a way that leads to a planned and well-expressed response.

- Using two or more sources of information – The skill of using more than one source of information to successfully problem solve.

- Understanding Space – Understanding how space is a very important part of life and school and the root of both point of view and using directions.

- Selective Attention – The skill of identifying what is important in any situation and attending to what is necessary with appropriate focus.

- Making Comparisons – The act of spontaneously noting similarities and differences.

- Understanding Time – Understanding how time is a very important part of life and school.

Process – Elaborating Thought

- Problem Definition – The cognitive asset of being able to correctly define problems in a way that facilitates generating solutions efficiently and effectively.

63

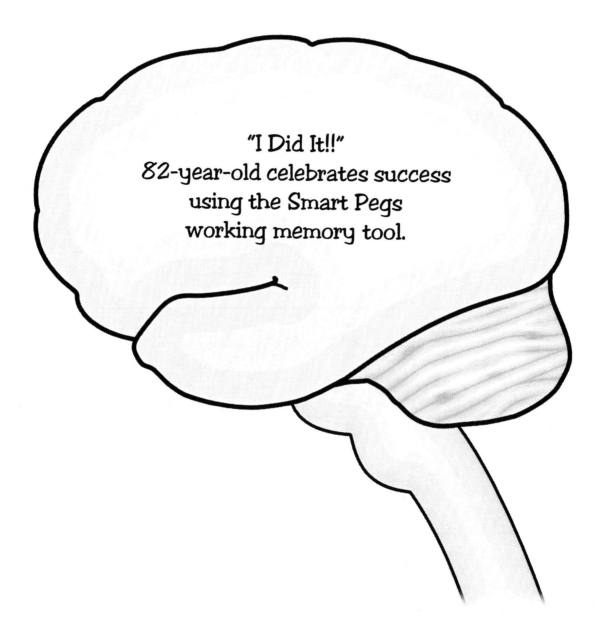

"I Did It!!"
82-year-old celebrates success
using the Smart Pegs
working memory tool.

- Classification - The capacity to compare, group, and systematically organize information according to one's purpose.

- Making Connections – The skill and capacity to make links between different sources of information in a way that creates deeper meaning and understanding.

- Systematic Planning – Appropriate planning behavior that is organized in a way that leads to a well-expressed response.

- Cognitive Flexibility – The skill and capacity for accurately assessing situations and adjusting thoughts and actions appropriately.

- Using Cues Appropriately – The ability to use necessary information given in the world to solve academic and life problems.

- Making Inferences/Hypothetical Thinking — The ability to solve problems and create new information by making inferences based on the information given and to go beyond what is said to a logical conclusion that is not explicit.

- Working Memory – The skill of consciously choosing what to retain in long-term memory and selecting appropriate tools to retain and recall information to achieve desired results.

- Making Meaning – The ability to access past experiences, connect with the new, and infuse an appropriate amount of energy into the learning experience knowing that it is important to life.

- Summarizing – The behavior of identifying what is most salient and important and communicating it in a verbal or written form in a succinct way.

Output – Applying in the World

- Point of View – Appropriate understanding and respect for other people's point of view that manifests itself in empathy and rapport.

- Thoughtful Behavior – The ability to stop, think, and respond in a manner that is appropriate in the situation.

- Effective Expression – A thoughtful response made after adequate exploration and planning is completed.

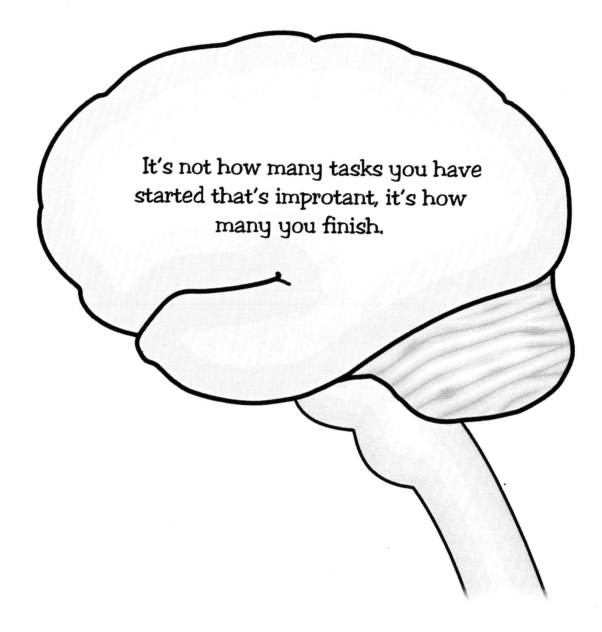

It's not how many tasks you have started that's improtant, it's how many you finish.

- Appropriate Courage – Appropriate courage is the cognitive asset of assessing situations, being clear on mission and goals, and taking appropriate action.

- Finishing Power – Appropriate task completion behavior that is sustained over time and in spite of difficulty.

- Learning from Experience - The skill of reflecting on experience and selecting what to do in the same way or differently the next time.

You will tend to
find what you're
looking for.
Think before you seek.

Chapter 6

Input: Seeing with New Eyes

When you treat
60,000 sparkling seconds
as the diamonds of your waking
day, you truly understand time.

Introduction

It is during the input phase that students show curiosity about seeking information in the world and then proceed to gather that information. When cognitive assets at the input phase have been coached and are in place in an individual's life, the student tends to show a curiosity about what exists in the world, appreciates that there are problems to be solved, and is able to gather an appropriate amount as well as the proper quality of information to solve problems.

In order to conceptualize the importance of the input phase and cognitive assets within it, consider the following two groups of students. In the first group, think of those who perhaps are known as very "good," that is, those who are quiet and often are said to be withdrawn; do not tend to show initiative; and seem to have a general lack of curiosity about the world around them. Now, in the second group, consider the students who show another set of qualities, which include seeming to be somewhat lacking in selective attention, seeking numerous and varied stimulation often; and seeming to gather many different types of information but often focusing on each bit only for a very short amount of time.

Although students in the second group are often the focus of disciplinary action at school, neither group is guided to develop the necessary cognitive assets at the input phase. In fact, when teachers learn about the three phases of genius and the importance of cognitive assets, they report concern that cognitive assets at the input phase are not being taught at school. It seems as if educators overlook these important skills and assume that students come to school with a full complement of cognitive assets necessary to do their schoolwork.

At the same time, the vision of a school where these assets are taught and learned is so compelling that many of our graduate students begin to teach these assets right away. These teachers have every intention of ensuring that their students will be able to sustain a clear sense of what they want to learn in each situation, approach each lesson with an attitude of practical optimism, use their initiative to learn beyond the lesson, systematically search for new information and knowledge about the lesson, listen with focused attention when necessary, manage their time well, and understand and use space for maximum learning.

After teachers discover the importance of the three phases of genius, they begin to see how to diagnose student difficulties in work and behavior. In workshops and graduate courses, teachers quickly see that the core of many student mistakes is trouble at the input level. Most often, students have not

Often when students have difficulty problem solving in school and life, it is because they do not have necessary input skill in place yet.

used their cognitive assets well at the input phase, ending up with a low grade on tests or class assignments during the output phase. The input problem results in both processing and output difficulties, which show up as a low grade.

In the three phases of genius model, it is during the input phase that the senses gather necessary sensory information that becomes "grist for the mill" for thinking. The human brain gathers information through the traditional five senses, with the three most often used at school being the visual, auditory, and kinesthetic-tactile systems. Today, researchers believe that there are more than the traditional five senses as well. Each of the brain's lobes does its particular information-gathering job. For example, the occipital lobe specializes in visual input and processing, whereas specialized areas in the temporal lobes are responsible for hearing.

Some children enter and proceed through school with input skills well in place. For example, some students have learned to focus and listen well; some have an understanding of space so that they are not intrusive or distant and use space appropriately on paper; some have an adequate understanding of time; and some have learned the importance of gathering all needed information when problem solving. However, we believe that these input skills need to be taught at school, not just in the home. Three primary reasons support our position. First, many students do not enter school with these types of input phase cognitive assets in place. The students who do not have these skills in place arrive in all types of classes: regular education, special education, and gifted programs.

The second reason that cognitive assets need to be taught at all three phases is that we are no longer living in the industrial age, but rather in the age of information, which is defined by the need for learning, education, knowledge awareness, and technology. Students have massive amounts of information to process during each hour of their day. Therefore, it is important that we have a model for understanding how learning happens. With such a model in place we are able to intervene and improve learning and thinking. The third reason for teaching input skills at school is that, although they are critically necessary for student achievement in school, they are not taught to students. In neither workshops nor graduate studies have we heard teachers articulate the belief that input skills are covered at school adequately enough that students are able to improve their educational outcomes as a result. However, teachers report that when they begin to teach the cognitive assets at the input phase, students exhibit a greater positive range of behaviors and achieve at higher levels. Now, let us examine three important input skills mentioned earlier.

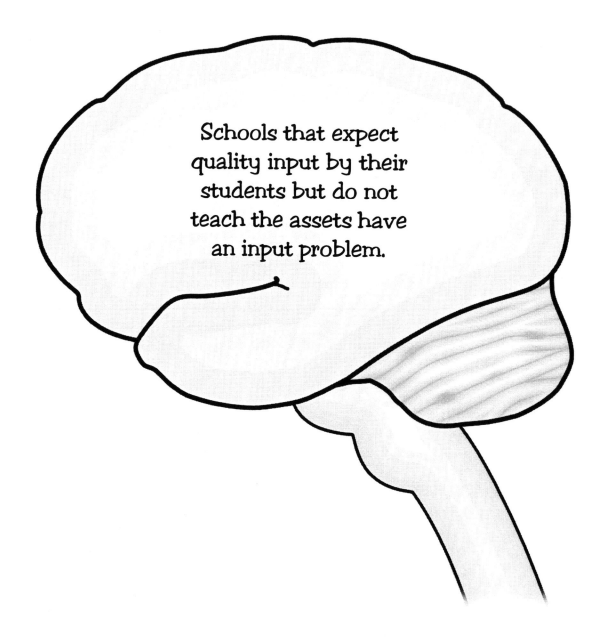

Schools that expect
quality input by their
students but do not
teach the assets have
an input problem.

Initiative – Example 1

Studies suggest that the single most important characteristic of people who are stars at work is that they demonstrate initiative. This cognitive asset is treasured by successful companies because people with initiative achieve far superior levels of productivity. The same is true for students at school. Those students who take the initiative to read the chapter of a book that relates to a lesson they are going to have the next day tend to learn much more from the lesson than those students who do not use initiative to prepare for class. In the same way, teachers who take the initiative to learn new research about the brain and learning and then apply strategies in their classrooms tend to achieve better results with their students. We have included this important cognitive asset at the input phase and, in fact, believe that it is often actually a prerequisite for gathering necessary information.

Systematic Search – Example 2

Do you know people who limit their life possibilities and progress because of impulsive behavior? After learning how to use the cognitive asset of systematic search, many students' impulsive behaviors begin to decrease.

Consider another use of systematic search. Consider the problem of life stress and how to decrease it. By some estimates, stress costs the U.S. economy around $100 billion a year in lost productivity. It can cause havoc on the immune system and reduce the enjoyment of life. By using the cognitive asset of systematic search, one can gather information from the Internet, bookstore, and library about the latest research on stress and create action plans for stress reduction. Then, it is possible to start putting this together in your life.

Understanding Space – Example 3

Have you ever had a student who does not understand space, or its companion, directions? Often, they have trouble with the understanding of relative space—right, left, back, and front. Or have you ever received, or given, directions that didn't result in successful navigation?

Most teachers agree that both an understanding of space and time are essential cognitive assets if students are to perform well at school. Both of these cognitive assets vary greatly among cultures; thus, they must be explained and coached if culturally different students are to have equal opportunities to excel within the school culture. For example, if students do not understand and use space as it is used within the school culture, they might appear to be detached if they stand too far apart, or to be fighting if they get too close to each other. Furthermore, teachers often see written products where space is not used properly, resulting in illegible papers.

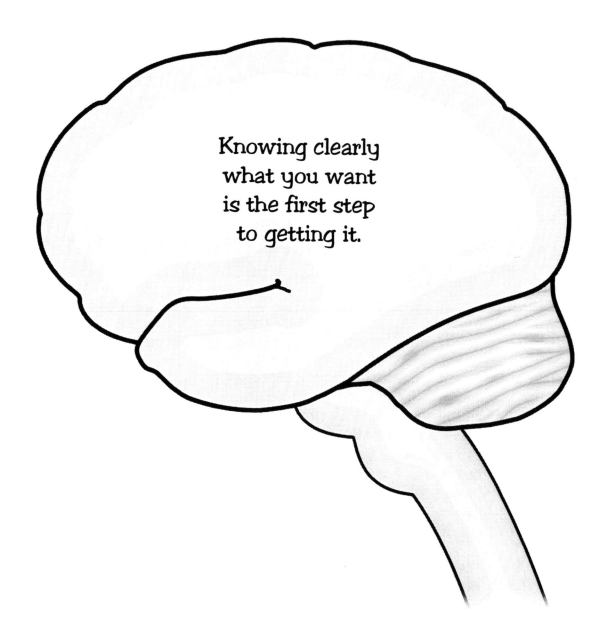

Knowing clearly
what you want
is the first step
to getting it.

Input Phase: Nine Cognitive Assets

☼ Cognitive Asset: Clear Intent

Our Challenge: "I have students who lack motivation and who do not have a clear intent about what they want."

Definition: Sustaining a clear sense of what one's intentions are in each situation. For example, the teacher who has the clear intention of increasing student learning by constantly improving their instructional skills will tend to increase their effectiveness and achieve their goals.

Teacher Intent: To help students gain a sense of clear intent about their goals in their daily school and family lives.

Have you met people who seem to know what they want in each situation? Such individuals are effective at applying the cognitive asset of clear intent. Have you also met people who seem to meander aimlessly through life and are unclear about what they want? Their lack of clear intent keeps them from focusing their energy on steps that move them towards their goals. The great news is that we can cultivate the cognitive asset of clear intent in ourselves and others.

Clear Intent: A Sample Lesson

Ask students to practice asking the following questions:

Step 1: What do I want ?

Step 2: Why do I want it?

Step 3: When do I want it?

Step 4: How will I know when I have achieved it?

Step 5: How does this goal lead me to a greater mission?

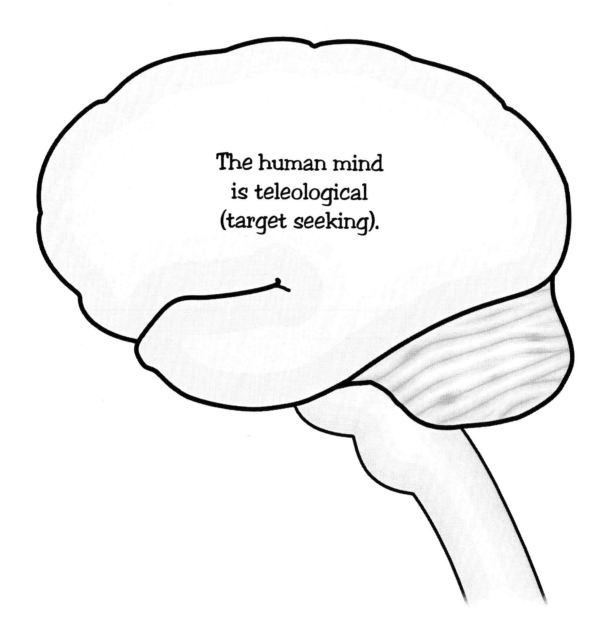

The human mind
is teleological
(target seeking).

Sample Guiding Questions
W.I.N.

What's Important Now?
What's my Intention Now?
What Impact am I having Now?

A Story of Clear Intent in Action

Marcus will always remember the thrill of seeing the moon landing and going to see some moon rocks at a museum in Cambridge, England. When President Kennedy stated that he wanted to get a man on the moon and safely back again in 10 years, he was modeling a great example of clear intent. When you look for them, you will see great examples of this in everyday life and in the classroom. You can often tell if someone has clear intent because they are very clear in describing what they want. This asset can also be seen in highly focused behavior, as can be seen in the following story.

> *Marcus was working in a fully inclusive classroom that had many students with learning challenges. One little boy who had significant neurological challenges was focusing all his energy on trying to type something on the computer. Every move was difficult but he just kept typing. Eventually, he smiled with delight. His teacher clapped. He had succeeded in typing his new second name. He had just been adopted.*

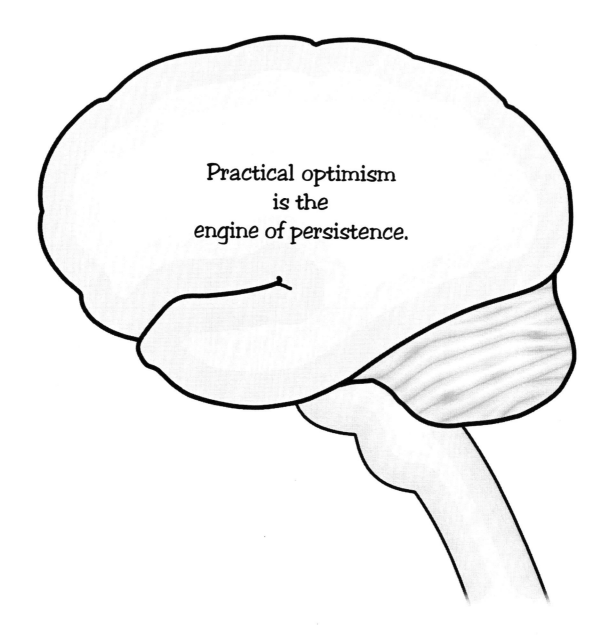

Practical optimism
is the
engine of persistence.

⚲ Cognitive Asset: Practical Optimism

Our Challenge: "We have students who stop trying when they experience failure. They feel they fail because they are dumb and it is not worth the effort to keep trying."

Definition: An approach to life that focuses on taking practical positive action to increase the probability of successful outcomes.

Teacher Intent: To model and mediate an attitude of practical optimism in everyday classroom language and behavior.

A growing body of research confirms that optimism is a key predictor of high academic achievement, health, happiness, and career success. At the same time, optimism is a great defense against depression, which is reaching an epidemic level in the United States today. One Harvard researcher found that up to 23% of young people had suffered from some form of depression.

The wonderful finding is that optimism can be learned and can transform how educators can think about creating a positive classroom climate. Now, we can systematically work at cultivating the cognitive asset of practical optimism among our students and colleagues so that we can support healthy thinking and high academic achievement. For example, West Point began to use an instrument to assess optimism as a predictor of who would drop out. They discovered that the most optimistic cadets were the least likely to drop out and that the most pessimistic cadets were the most likely to do so. In studies about the impact of optimism in the classroom, it was discovered that students who were most pessimistic tended to give up when facing difficult or impossible tasks. They also seemed to internalize that the problem was that they were not smart enough and that the situation would not improve. In *Thinking for Results*, we use the I-4 model to map the thinking process so that we can intervene in a way that can improve optimism.

Practical Optimism: A Sample Lesson

Step 1: Look at the I-4 model that illustrates the flow of thought: Information, Interpretation, Impact, and Influence.

Step 2: Consider some Information that might impact you. For example, you get a bad grade.

Step 3: Consider your Interpretation of this. For example you might think, "I did not do enough work to get a good grade."

81

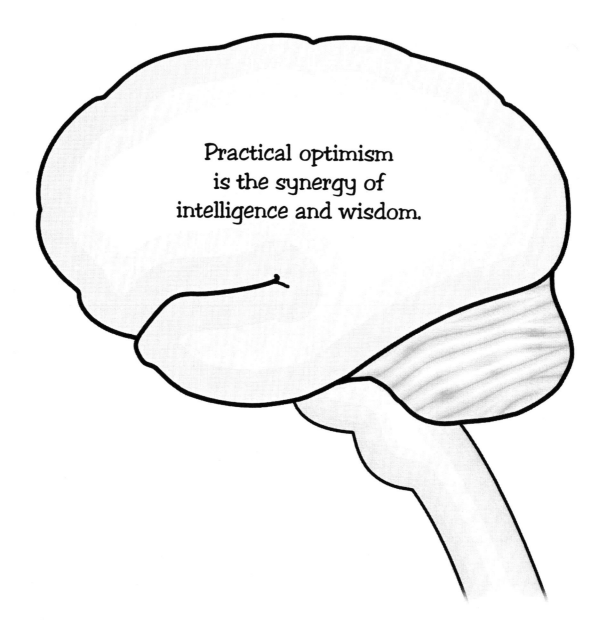

Practical optimism
is the synergy of
intelligence and wisdom.

Step 4: Consider the Impact of this thought. For example, you might feel disappointed about your grade.

Step 5: Consider how you can Influence your grades. For example, you might choose to do the paper again; do more research; or plan the next paper differently.

Step 6: Change some of the variables in the above. For example, that the information you get is that you get a good grade.

Step 7: On an ongoing basis, use this framework to analyze your thinking.

Sample Guiding Questions

What is the *Information* I am receiving?
What is my *Interpretation* of this information?
What is the *Impact* on how I feel and think?
What can I do to positively *Influence* the situation?

A Story of Practical Optimism

There was once a BrainSMART teacher who was concerned that many of her students were not optimistic when they faced failure. She decided that her students needed to have some concrete experiences of success around reading. She decided to use a range of strategies to increase the probability of them doing well and at the same time she chose a motivating story to work on. She used the story, The Swan and the Trumpet. She used BrainWEBS to introduce the story; Storyscapes to bring the story to life' and a variety of other tools. When she finished the lessons, virtually all of the students scored over 90% in reading comprehension. More importantly, they internalized the concrete feeling of success.

This story illustrates the fuel of optimism. The information the students received was one that they had done well on their reading assignment. Their interpretation could be they had done well because they used great strategies. The impact could be that they felt successful. The influence was that in the future they could be optimistic about reading.

83

Initiative is key to beginning the problem solving process. People who show initiative appropriately are more successful in life and work.

♀ Cognitive Asset: Initiative

Our Challenge: "Some of my students do not begin tasks on their own. They seem to always need a jump-start from the teacher."

Definition: Readiness and skill in taking action.

Teacher Intent: To model and mediate personal and professional initiative.

What is it like to work with someone who goes above and beyond what is expected to take a proactive step towards making your work life more productive? Have you noticed that some people take the initiative in protecting their health by learning about risk factors, for example, factors affecting the risk of heart disease? They might reduce the amount of saturated fats in their diet, exercise more, and eat more fiber. Research suggests that people who reduce such risk factors may have a longer life expectancy.

In your classroom, you may notice that some students are keen to initiate projects or make links between what you have taught them and events they see in the world. Other students, however, have not cultivated the asset of initiative and may simply wait passively for instructions about what to do.

Research suggests that initiative is the single most important asset for success at work. For example, highly effective teachers who attend workshops and read books are keen to implement new ideas. Such teachers can dramatically increase student achievement. The asset of initiative is often the difference between success and failure in one's personal and professional life.

Initiative: A Sample Lesson

Step 1:   Ask your students to consider characters in their favorite TV show or movie who take appropriate risks to show initiative to accomplish tasks.

Step 2:   Ask the students what their chosen characters do that shows initiative.

Step 3:   Ask them to consider what happens in the character's life as a result of their initiative.

Step 4:   Ask the students to reflect and consider when they need to use initiative at school.

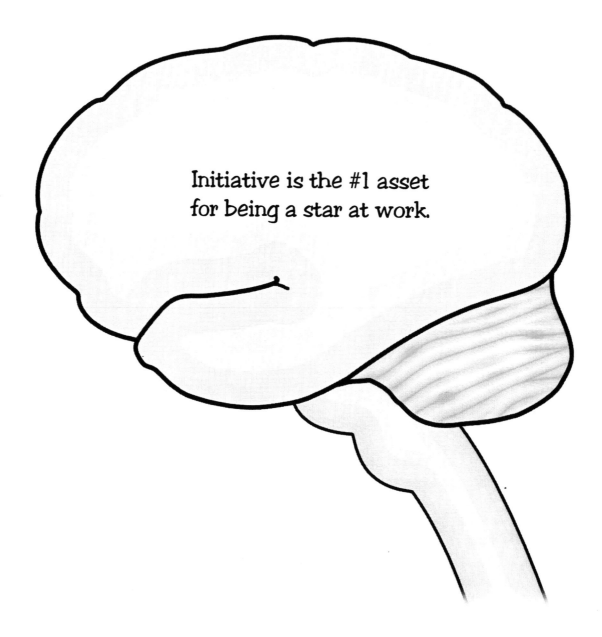

Initiative is the #1 asset for being a star at work.

Sample Guiding Questions

Who is a role model for me in terms of *showing initiative*?

What is my *clear intent* in this situation?

Given that I am responsible for my actions, what do I need to do to "start the ball rolling" so that I can *actualize my clear intentions*?

A Story of Initiative in Action

A critical aspect of leadership is to lead by example and demonstrate initiatives that others follow. One BrainSMART graduate student was keen to help her own children become skilled at taking the initiative to get their homework completed. In order to facilitate this result, this graduate student and mother took the initiative and lead by example. Although she lacked some computer and Internet experiences, she took the proactive steps of spending time online to complete assignments for her graduate degree and to research exciting ideas. She became obviously enthusiastic about her new activities. She went beyond what was expected for completion of her assignment and showed initiative in learning more broadly and more deeply. The result of this powerful modeling of initiative was that her own children became skilled at starting their homework in the evenings, getting it completed, and going beyond what they had been asked to do.

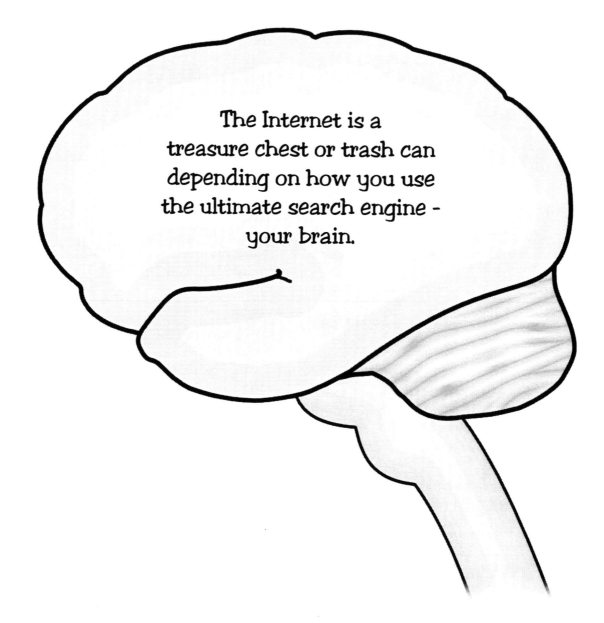

The Internet is a treasure chest or trash can depending on how you use the ultimate search engine - your brain.

💡 Cognitive Asset: Systematic Search

Our Challenge: "I have impulsive students showing up in my class that don't even know how to begin to do a simple lesson!"

Definition: Appropriate exploratory behavior that is organized in a way that leads to a planned and well expressed response.

Teacher Intent: To facilitate a need within the student to use an organized method to gather resources for solving any problem in life and school. As guide, the teacher amplifies the *process* of gathering data in an organized way.

Most of us would agree that being skilled at systematically solving problems is not something that we are able to do innately at birth. It is a learned skill. However, many students come to school without this skill and, as with many other necessary skills, it is not taught explicitly as a skill that most everyone can further develop. We teach problem solving in three phases: (a) systematic search, (b) planning, and (c) controlling self-expression. All need to be used systematically and habitually for maximum benefit. To teach students how to systematically solve a problem, notice the sample lesson with steps for teaching students how to accomplish systematic search.

Systematic Search: A Sample Lesson

Step 1:   As a class, discuss what it means to gather information about a problem. How does good problem solving include this phase of the process? How is this different from impulsive action?

Step 2:   As a class, choose a topic as an example to study, i.e. healthy eating.

Step 3:   Create a mind map of ways to gather information about the topic. (For more information about mind mapping and other visual techniques see *BrainSMART Strategies for Boosting Test Scores* (2000). Examples from students might be to get a book on nutrition, go to a wellness doctor, take a class at the health department, ask a very healthy person, or explore it on the Internet.

Step 4:   Ask students the following question: How can we use what we have learned about gathering information in Language Arts, or other classes, today? How can we gather information in our lives?

Remember the saying,
"Garbage In = Garbage Out"
Gathering information accurately
is critical for good problem solving.

Step 5: After students have had a chance to gather information, ask them to work in pairs and share how they accomplished the task.

Sample Guiding Questions

What are the *resources* available to me to solve the problem?
What *materials* do I need to complete this exercise?
How do I *plan* to gather the necessary information for this paper?

When we have taught students in this process-oriented approach, they have often said that it helps show them the way to be successful. With the emphasis on grades and tests, younger students often think that the only aspect of problem solving is *expression*, the last phase. Until thinking class, they often do not know that the care with which we gather information and make a plan often determine the outcome after expression!

When we have trained teachers using this approach, they think it is exciting and see that it makes a difference! Often these courageous teachers are surprised to see how focused educational systems seem to be on the product, rather than the process. We believe, along with many other teachers, that student products get better when students understand the process leading to the development of the product or expression of knowledge.

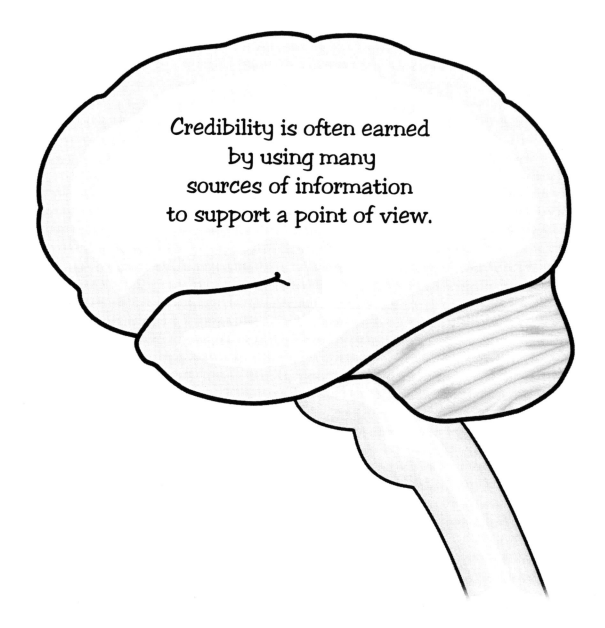

Credibility is often earned
by using many
sources of information
to support a point of view.

💡 Cognitive Asset: Using Two or More Sources of Information

Our Challenge: "I have students in my class that only use one source at a time. For example, on book reports they include ideas from one book."

Definition: The skill of using more than one source of information to successfully solve problems.

Teacher Intent: To model and mediate the asset of using two or more sources of information to reach conclusions and solve problems.

We live in a time when the volume of information available is growing at an almost exponential rate. However, availability of information by itself does not guarantee learning or success. It is the ability to acquire, validate, and apply information that adds value. This is equally true in our personal and profession lives. For example, imagine you are thinking about buying a car. One way is just to go to a car dealer and ask them questions. A second possibility would be to read a consumer report about the car before you go to a dealership. A third possibility might be to get information about the vehicle from someone you know who has the same sort of car as the one you are interested in. As you can see, getting information from more than one source can help you make better decisions.

Consider the importance of using two or more sources to understand different viewpoints in history. For example, if you had asked an Englishman, such as Cornwallis, what he thought about the revolution in the Americas, he might have a different set of information to give you than George Washington. By gathering information from two or more sources, one can get a more multidimensional view on a subject.

Using Two or More Sources of Information: A Sample Lesson

Step 1:   Ask your students to think about how they could write a report about fast foods in America.

Step 2:   Ask students to predict what information might come from using only one source that we will call the American Fast Food Organization.

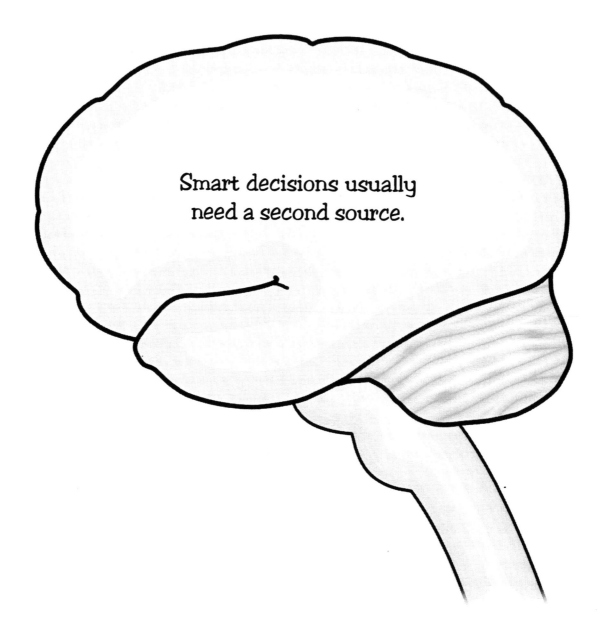

Smart decisions usually
need a second source.

Step 3: Ask students to brainstorm other sources of information that might build a more complete picture about the impact of fast food on America.

Step 4: Ask students to write a report based on using two or more sources of information.

Step 5: Review their work and then facilitate a discussion on the merits of getting many sources of information.

A Story About Using
Two or More Sources of Information

One day, Mary went to school full of joy. She loved meeting with her friends and socializing during lunch and on the bus on the way home. On this particular day, something happened that changed everything. Mary's best friend, Tammy, was walking across the cafeteria to the table where she and Mary almost always ate lunch. Today, however, Tammy just kept walking past the table and went to sit next to some other friends. Mary was surprised and walked over to Tammy and said "How are you doing?" "I don't want to talk to you after what you said about me," Tammy replied. "What do you mean?" said Mary. "You know," said Tammy and turned her back on Mary. Mary was distraught and went away feeling hurt and confused. Then it hit her. Tammy was sitting next to Diane, who was known to make things up in order to stir up things at school. Mary decided to do nothing. That afternoon, just as Mary was getting on the bus, Tammy ran up and said, "Mary, I am so sorry. Diane made up a lie about what you said about me. I just did not think to check it out with anyone else. I was only using one source of information. Then I asked some other friends, and they told me that Diane just lied in order to get you and me to fight."

95

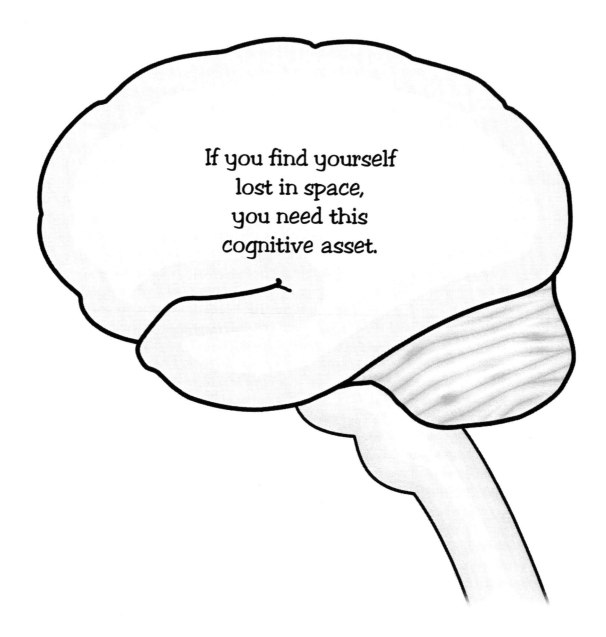

If you find yourself
lost in space,
you need this
cognitive asset.

♀ Cognitive Asset: Understanding Space

Our Challenge: "A lot of our students get in trouble because they get in other people's personal space in a disrespectful way."

Definition: Understanding how space is a very important part of life and school.

Teacher Intent: To facilitate the students' need and skill to be able to get around in the world in a successful way. As guide, the teacher amplifies the *process* of understanding spatial concepts.

In his new book, *A Biological Brain in a Cultural Classroom*, Sylwester (2000) notes that space and time are important issues in classroom management. Ask any teacher how important it is for learners to be able to navigate through space without bumping into others, and the importance of the use of space when constructing a work of art. This is core understanding that students need to grasp point of view of self as well as of other.

Understanding Space: A Sample Lesson

Step 1: As I gently bump into the door facing me, I ask the students, "Am I using space concepts well at the moment?"

Step 2: The students will often laugh as I frame the lesson as my mistake. I might question, "Do any of you ever have difficulty like me because of a problem with use of space concepts?"

Step 3: Ask the class, "What are some problems that can occur as a result?"

Step 4: After they have had a chance to reflect and answer the question, I often ask, "How do we use space concepts when we do paper or computer work?"

Step 5: Here it is useful to encourage careful examination of spacing procedures and readability of papers.

Step 6: Encourage students to consider their use of space in the classroom and in their lives elsewhere.

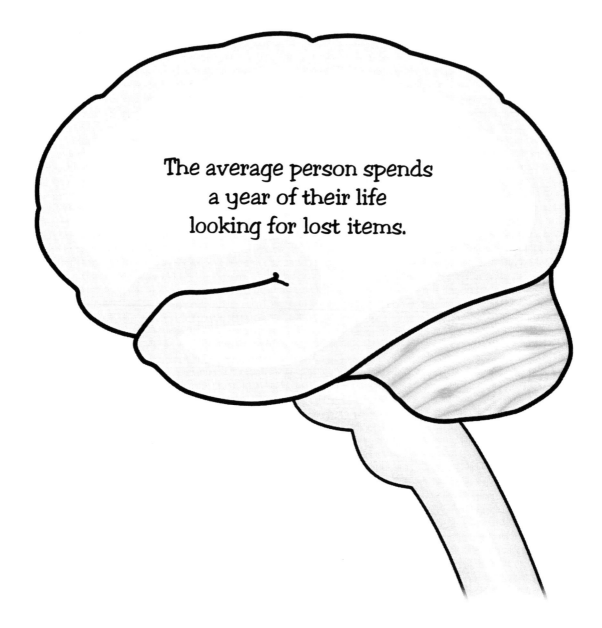

The average person spends
a year of their life
looking for lost items.

Billy's Story

"I didn't know that space concepts were so important until we studied them in thinking class. Now, I use space in the cafeteria line and don't get in trouble for bumping people in the line. My papers are neater. I make rows when I write and my teacher says she can read it better. My mother uses space concepts when she drives. She always keeps space after other cars in front of us. It is fun to be studying something so important for people all ages."

Sample Guiding Questions

Am I being *offensive* to others by standing too close when I'm in conversation them?
Do my papers indicate that my *writing* is too "squeezed together" or "spaced out" to be read clearly?
What does *spatial orientation* have to do with point of view?
How is this *important* in literature?
How is this *important* in war history?

Many believe that today we live in an attention economy. Those students that master attention will do well.

💡 Cognitive Asset: Selective Attention

Our Challenge: "Many students arrive in classrooms without the cognitive assets for sustaining focused attention on learning tasks."

Definition: The skill of identifying what is important in any situation and attending to what is necessary with appropriate focus.

Teacher Intent: To model and mediate the skill of choosing what to focus attention on in order to achieve important goals.

Some researchers believe that we are now living in what they call "the attention economy." Those who succeed and thrive in this new paradigm are those who cultivate skills in investing their attention wisely. For example, to be an effective teacher, it is critical that primary attention be given to the tasks that raise student achievement. Less effective teachers waste their attention on irrelevant information such as students' socioeconomic backgrounds and appearance.

The reality of the attention economy is that students face a barrage of media messages designed to hook their attention, get their brand loyalty, and ultimately take their money. For example, students see thousands of television commercials and online advertising messages. To compete with this, teachers need to cultivate student assets of selective attention so that higher levels of academic learning can be achieved in spite of many potential distractions.

Selective Attention: A Sample Lesson

Step 1: Ask your students to do an internet search on a particular topic.

Step 2: After they have had a chance to do their search, ask them if they had any trouble staying on the topic of the search.

Step 3: Ask your students to tell the group what strategies they use to stay on task when they search, in other words, how do they use selective attention when they do an internet search.

Step 4: As always when you guide your students, amplify the strategies that work.

Step 5: Ask your students when they need to use selective attention to accomplish other tasks at school or home.

101

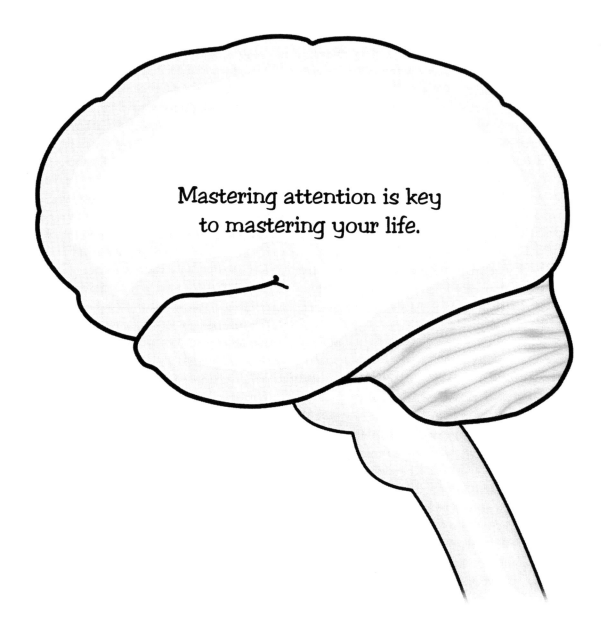

Mastering attention is key
to mastering your life.

Sample Guiding Questions

What do I need to attend to so that I can
actualize my clear intent in this situation?
Is there something that I must choose to ignore
so that I can attend to specific stimuli?
W.hat's I.mportant N.ow! Furthermore, what do I need to
pay attention to in order to create win-win situations at school and in life?

A Story of
Selective Attention in Action

One highly effective teacher who works with at-risk middle school students found that few students arrived with the asset of selective attention. She saw the potential that these students had and realized potential could not translate to success unless this asset of selective attention was cultivated. Having seen one of the BrainSMART team present the H.E.A.R. strategy (See this strategy in BrainSMART 60 Strategies for Boosting Test Scores), she immediately brought it back to her classroom and shared it with her students. Because the strategy engages the kinesthetic system so well, she found that her students really enjoyed learning this tool for increasing selective attention. She found that the classroom climate and learning improved as students began to use the system on a regular basis. It became part of their culture of demonstrating respect by giving others full attention. The teacher also believes that learning the skill might have saved lives as some of the students were at-risk for gang activity where perceived disrespect by not giving attention could result in deadly consequences.

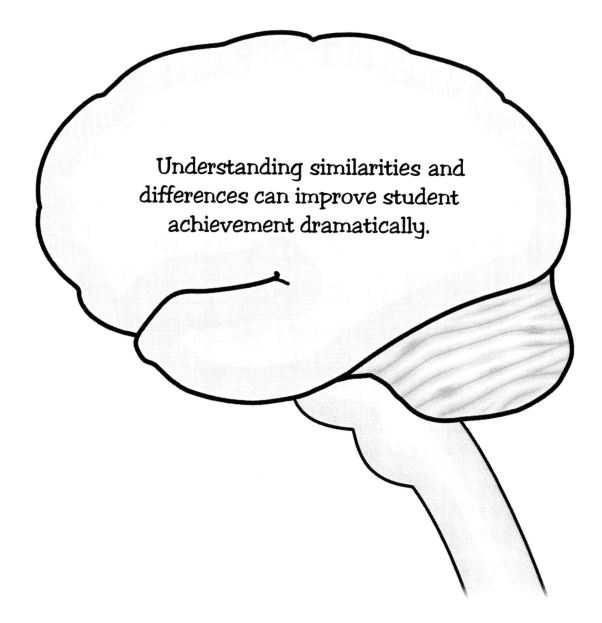

Understanding similarities and differences can improve student achievement dramatically.

🔅 Cognitive Asset: Making Comparisons

Our Challenge: "Many students arrive in our classrooms without the necessary assets for making useful comparisons between given data. At the same time, studies suggest that this capacity is critical for any higher level thinking to be possible."

Definition: The act of spontaneously noting similarities and differences.

Teacher Intent: To model and mediate the asset of making comparisons in any given content area and in life.

Research suggests that the skill of finding similarities and differences has significant impact on student achievement. When teachers conduct instruction in a way that cultivates this asset, students may achieve a 20% to 40% gain compared with students who do not receive such instruction. With practice, teachers can weave examples into their curriculum that strengthen this skill set.

Making Comparisons: A Sample Lesson

Step 1: Ask your students to name two of their favorite characters from books, T.V., or the movies.

Step 2: Next, ask them to compare these two characters.

Step 3: After introducing the idea of criteria, or principles of comparison, ask the students to articulate the criteria by which they are comparing.

Step 4: Based on chosen criteria, how are the characters similar?

Step 5: How are the characters different?

Step 6: Based on your exploration in this lesson, why do you think these characters are favorites of yours? Often this is a great time to discuss the issue of clear intent and talk about how our intentions and purpose drive our choice of criteria by which to compare. For example, if your intention is to learn more about ethical behavior and contribution to the world, you might compare by this criteria. If what is important to you is surface beauty, you might compare by this criteria.

105

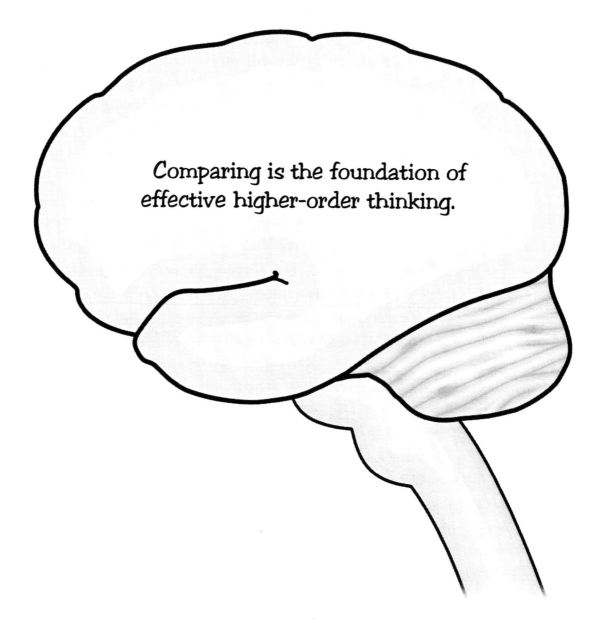

Comparing is the foundation of
effective higher-order thinking.

Sample Guiding Questions

In this situation what is my *clear intent*?
By what *criteria* am I comparing in order to action my intentionality?
What are the similarities and differences according to
my *criteria for comparisons*?

A Story of
Making Comparisons in Action

Many BrainSMART graduate students have been fascinated about the impact of nutrition on the performance of the body brain learning system. In particular, they have been intrigued by the impact of what is eaten at breakfast on the brain, learning, and energy level. For example, let us compare what many teachers do for breakfast with the nutrition that would sustain energy and enhance mood for a successful morning of teaching.

Imagine a teacher who gets up; is too rushed to have a nice breakfast; and downs a cup of coffee and a donut before leaving the house. Within an hour of teaching the energy begins to drain from her body. The sugary carbohydrate in the donut spiked her blood sugar for a short time, but now insulin has kicked in and she is quickly loosing energy. Her brain is screaming for glucose so she grabs another sugary snack, and her blood sugar plummets again leaving her feeling exhausted and in a low mood.

Now, imagine a teacher who, instead, applies her knowledge of the body brain system by eating smart. First, she wakes up her system with up to 30 grams of protein in any form she likes. This immediately starts to boost her dopamine and norepenephrine. This gives her energy; lifts her mood; and sharpens her focus for a fabulous morning of teaching. Then the high fiber cereal that she ate after eating protein helped her to stay full for longer and kept her blood sugar at an optimum level. Third, the fruits she also consumed gave her a health protecting dose of vitamin C and a slow release of glucose throughout the morning. Interestingly, some studies suggest that people who regularly consume a healthy breakfast live up to three years longer.

107

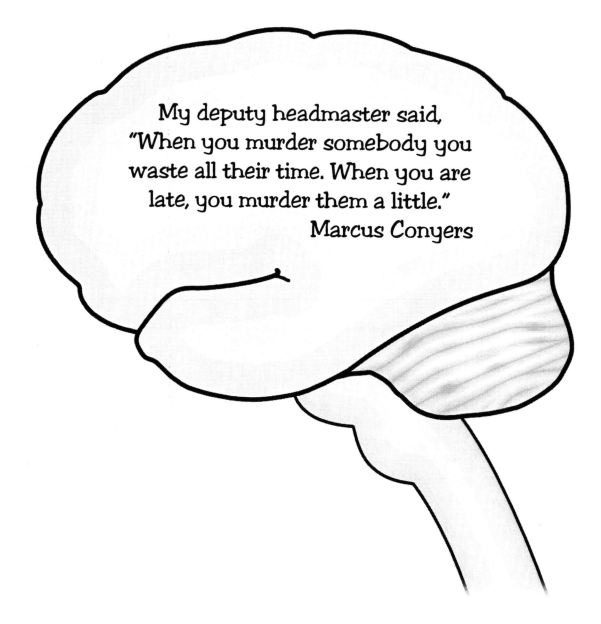

My deputy headmaster said, "When you murder somebody you waste all their time. When you are late, you murder them a little."
Marcus Conyers

💡 Cognitive Asset: Understanding Time

Our Challenge: "Many of our students have no concept of time. They are often late to class and late turning in their papers."

Definition: Understanding how time is a very important part of life and school.

Teacher Intent: To facilitate the students' need and skill at understanding time so that they will be able to be successful. As guide, the teacher amplifies the *process* of understanding time concepts.

More than many concepts, both organization of time and space must be mediated, or coached, because they have a strong cultural component. For example, reflect on this question: What child could learn how to use time to their benefit in relationships and to reach goals without some guidance about how this is done within the culture? It is important to help students begin to feel a sense of time as a part of understanding it. Also, it is necessary to help them use experiences to understand that time is subject to emotions. For example, it seems to fly or drag depending on one's emotional state. Given this, is it smart for learners to wear a timepiece and notice it?

Understanding Time: A Sample Lesson

Step 1:   Look at your watch and make a big deal of the time. Ask the students "What does 1 minute feel like?"

Step 2:   Give students a chance to answer.

Step 3:   Ask them to experiment with you and experience the way time feels different when we are and are not busy.

Step 4:   Tell the students that you are going to give them 1 minute of time with their eyes closed for quiet time. Ask them to please raise their hand when they think 1 minute has lapsed.

Step 5:   After you make a big deal of the differences for different students (it has always happened for groups of students), you set it up again.

Step 6:   This time give them a task to help develop habitual behavior, for example, a drill, over something they have learned. Ask them to respond as rapidly as possible.

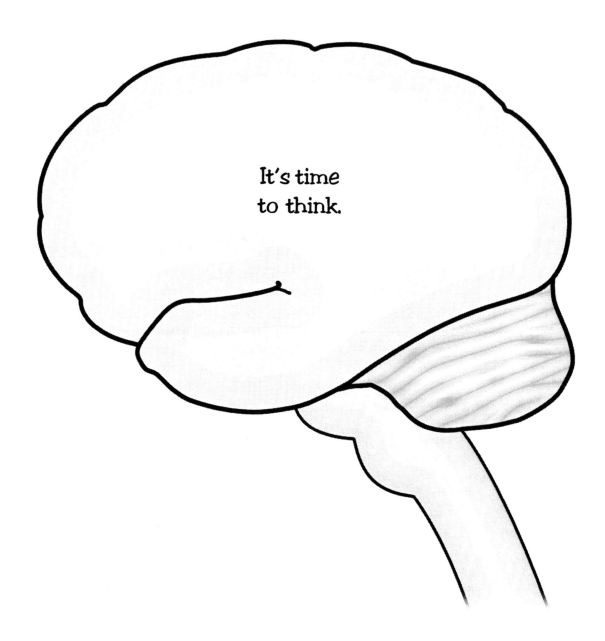

It's time
to think.

Step 7: Again, make a big deal of the start time and ask them to time themselves again with their internal clock while working and raise a hand when they think 1 minute is over.

Step 8: Afterward, discuss the emotional aspect of keeping track of time and the need for timepieces.

Step 9: As a whole group, ask students to give examples of problems they have experienced when they forgot to pay attention to this important aspect of life.

Sample Guiding Questions

Do I often get in trouble for *being late*?
How am I doing at *paying attention to time* when it is necessary?
Do I *use a timepiece* to check time when I have a deadline to meet?
Am I *pacing myself* well on tests?

Messing about with
ideas is the high road
to clear thinking.

Chapter 7

Processing: The Alchemy of Messing About

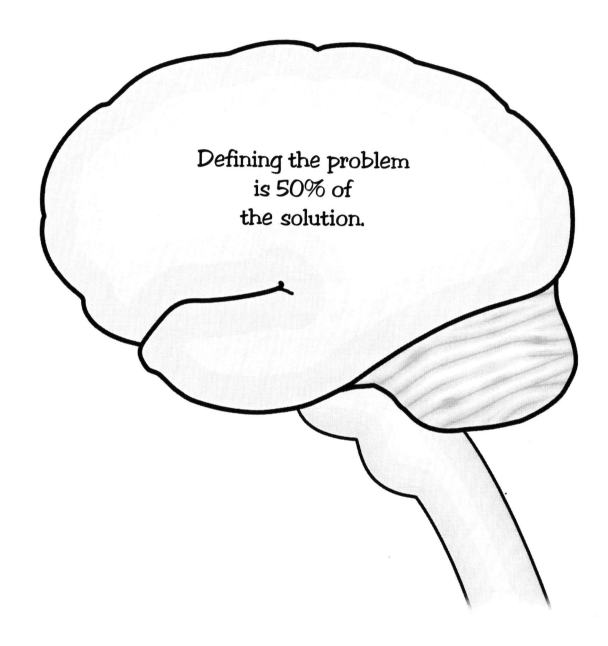

Defining the problem
is 50% of
the solution.

Introduction

The second phase of our model for developing necessary cognitive assets is called the processing phase. It is in this phase that we elaborate upon information gathered in the input phase. It is primarily within the processing phase that gathered information becomes our own. For example, consider the cognitive asset of working memory. It is by virtue of this asset that new information gathered in the input phase merges with memorable learning events in long-term memory storage to create new knowledge that may later be applied in the world in the output stage.

Graduate students and teachers in workshops have reported that occasionally cognitive assets within the processing phase are woven into the content of reading. Examples of this are when reading teachers work with students on making meaning and summarizing stories. However, it is very important to note some critical differences in what we know about the cognitive assets within reading instruction and what we are advocating in the Thinking for Results model. First, the power within the Thinking for Results approach exists because we see results in many areas of life and school when the assets are applied. Second, it is important that the assets be taught systematically and as a whole, not just in one content area such as reading. Third, it is critical that areas within the processing phase be coached as a part of the three phases of genius model, not as a stand-alone phase. Having mentioned these three differences, we want to say that the use of the three-phase model and cognitive assets within the content area of reading provides a powerful way to coach both reading and thinking. You also may be thinking of other isolated cognitive assets within the processing phase that are often taught in a subject matter area. An example might be the cognitive asset of making inferences and using hypothetical thinking that is often taught explicitly within the content of science at school.

A current and common problem that exists at the processing phase is that there are many students who have not had an opportunity outside of school to develop adequate language skills for processing. These students may have adequate or even sharply honed skills at the input phase, but have not had much practice or opportunity to interact with a learning guide or coach to develop the cognitive assets at the processing level. This problem may result in insufficient elaboration at the output level in verbal or written responses, or both.

Making Comparisons—Example 1

Research suggests that being able to compare information can lead to far higher levels of academic achievement. In one meta-analysis by Mazano, the

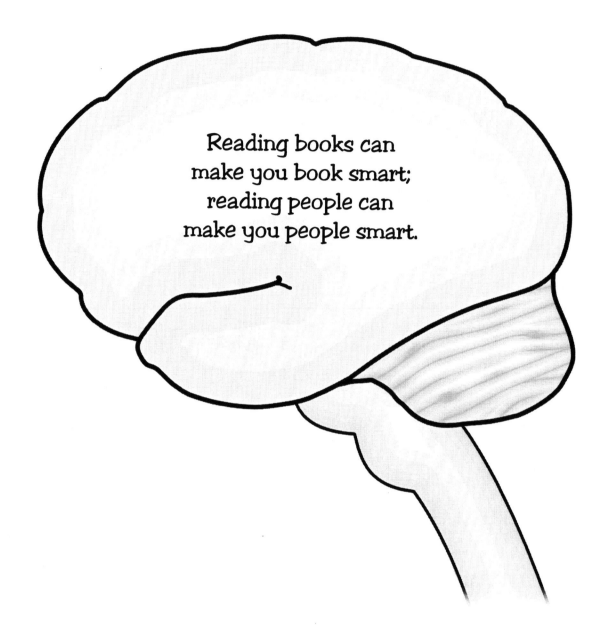

Reading books can
make you book smart;
reading people can
make you people smart.

percentile gain was 45% for students who used the cognitive asset of making comparisons to explore similarities and differences. In fact, skills of comparing, contrasting, and classifying can be thought of as part of the foundation for effective thinking.

For example, at a recent Learning and the Brain Conference, Marcus provided a workshop on the topic of the science of student achievement. To illustrate the power of the cognitive asset of making comparisons, he had the group in his workshop compare and contrast the U.S. Department of Agriculture's Food Pyramid and Harvard's Healthy Eating Pyramid. When the participants looked at the "use sparingly" category at the peak of the pyramids, they saw a dramatic difference. Harvard's Healthy Eating Pyramid suggested that we sparingly consume red meat, butter, and white flour. The participants quickly began to gain a deeper understanding of healthy nutrition by engaging in the cognitive work of comparing these two food pyramids.

Cognitive Flexibility—Example 2

Research suggests that the divorce rate for first-time marriages in the United States currently ranges between 50% and 60%. For second marriages, the divorce rate is even higher. Among those that remain happily married, evidence suggests that the cognitive asset of flexibility may be a factor. For example, a spouse who comes home after a hard day at work and habitually fails to shift his or her thinking away from the work life and into the family life may create difficulties in the home. Furthermore, the ability to change one's thinking, for example, to be open to the influence of your spouse for looking at things differently, can be a very positive contribution to a relationship and one's own mental health.

Systematic Planning—Example 3

When Donna taught the cognitive asset of systematic planning to a group of students in Delaware, the importance of this asset across all learners was amplified as participants gave real examples of when they need to use this important asset to succeed at school. In the group of fourth graders, many wanted to contribute to the class discussion on the topic. A boy who takes several foreign language courses after school commented that recently with his busy schedule he had forgotten some books he needed to finish his school work as well as work on his languages at home. Another child said that she needed to make a better plan for mornings so that she could consistently get to school on time each day. Indeed, the answers were varied and real from each corner of the room!

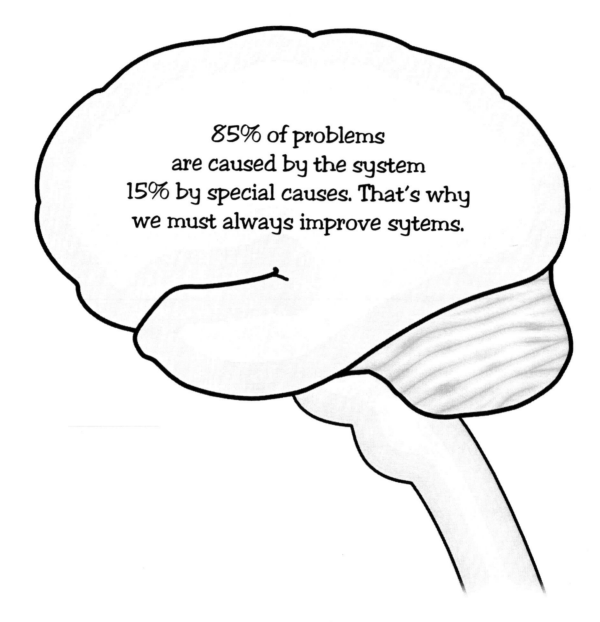

85% of problems
are caused by the system
15% by special causes. That's why
we must always improve sytems.

Processing Phase: Ten Cognitive Assets

♡ Cognitive Asset: Problem Definition

Our Challenge: "Our students do not know how to correctly define the problem. This means they often reach the wrong conclusions."

Definition: The cognitive asset of being able to correctly define problems in a way that facilitates generating solutions efficiently and effectively.

Teacher Intent: To model and mediate skill of correctly defining problems in a way that makes the problem-solving process transparent.

Voltaire said that no problem can withstand the assault of sustained thinking. The key first step to problem solving is to define the problem correctly. Many of life's challenges do not get solved because the problem is not defined correctly.

For example, in the United States there is a divorce rate of between 50% to 67%. Many people define the problem as being incompatibility or financial stress. With a 90% accuracy, researchers can now predict which couples will divorce based on observing their verbal and nonverbal communication (Gottman & Silver, 1999). More important, after the communication challenges are resolved and new communication skills learned the chances of successful marriage increase dramatically. So, if the problem is correctly defined as one of not learning the tools of effective communication, the solution becomes clear — teach communication skills. Another example is from education. Research suggests that the key to increasing student achievement is to improve instructional effectiveness of teachers. However if the problem is defined as the socioeconomic situation of the students and parents, then attention will not be centered on giving professional development and time to teachers. As with other cognitive assets, problem definition can be learned and taught.

Problem Definition: A Sample Lesson

Step 1: Ask students to think of a problem that faces their school.

Step 2: Ask your students to explain what the impact of this problem is.

Step 3: Ask you students to create a definition of what the problem is.

119

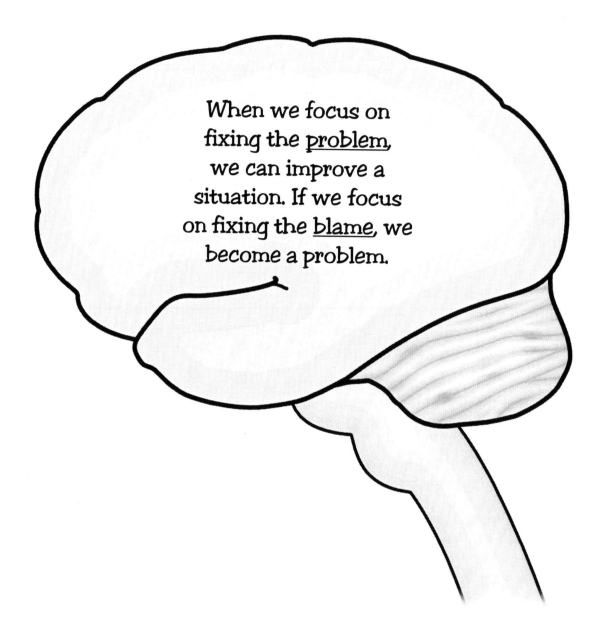

When we focus on fixing the <u>problem</u>, we can improve a situation. If we focus on fixing the <u>blame</u>, we become a problem.

Step 4. Ask them to generate another possible definition of what the problem is.

Step 5: Ask them to compare the two problem definitions and decide which is most probably accurate.

Step 6: Ask them to explain their decision.

Step 7: Ask them to suggest three possible solutions.

Step 8: Ask them to rank their ideas according to the probability of success.

Step 9: Ask students to explain their choice.

Questions for Problem Definition

What is the problem ?
How do I know it's a problem?
Who's problem is it?
What else could the problem be?
What are three *possible solutions*?
Which is *most* likely to be *effective*?

A Story About Problem Definition

Once upon a time in a far off land there lived a King who had two sons. He loved his sons dearly and could not choose who should take over his throne when he died. To settle the matter he arranged for the sons to race their camels across the desert from the hot, dry mountains all the way to the oasis. Whoever's <u>camel</u> would arrive <u>last</u> would win the crown. It was the day of the race, and the two sons kept going around in circles getting hotter and more and more tired trying to be the last one to the oasis. They were miserable and could not think of a solution. Then, they met a wise teacher who said something to the sons. They dismounted; got on the camels again; and with hoots of joy galloped towards the cool of the oasis. The solution? They had <u>switched</u> camels with each other. Since each was riding his brother's camel, they were determined to get to the oasis first so their own camel would arrive last.

121

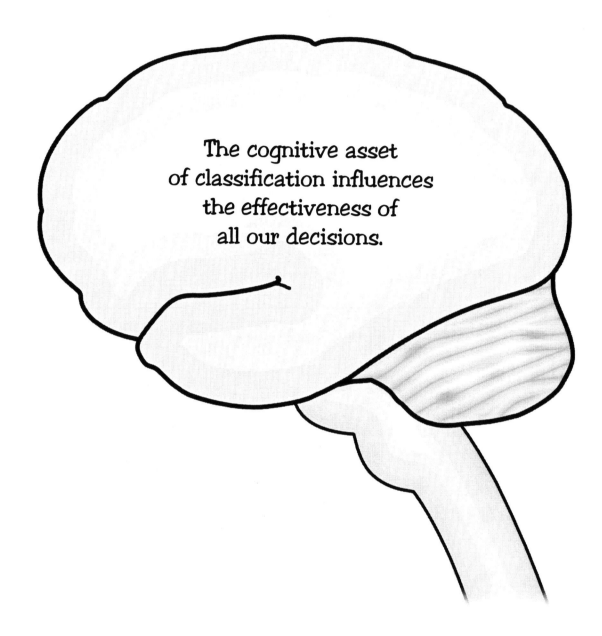

The cognitive asset
of classification influences
the effectiveness of
all our decisions.

♀ Cognitive Asset: Classification

Our Challenge: "We have students that do not classify information well so they waste a lot of time and do not obtain the correct answer."

Definition: The capacity to compare, group, and systematically organize information according to purpose.

Teacher Intent: To model and mediate the tools for comparing, grouping, and relating information.

The ascent of humankind may be linked to man's ability to classify effectively. Being able to classify which plants are safe to eat, which animals were best to hunt, which areas of land offer the best protection from the elements was key to survival. This cognitive asset allows human beings to organize their experiences of life into a way that they can learn and help them thrive. For example, when it comes to consuming foods that are nutrient rich and calorie poor it is essential to have an effective classification system to navigate the overwhelming choices available today. Marcus appeared on television in a segment about the BrainSMART/BodyWise grant from the Winter Park Health Foundation that was used to promote health at Brookshire Elementary school. The interviewer, at one point, stated that the guidelines classified ketchup as a "vegetable." In our workshops, we suggest the classification that "White Carbs Add Pounds." We mean that processed carbohydrates such as white bread, sugar, white pasta, potatoes, and others, add calories and may stimulate production of insulin, the fat storage hormone.

Classification: A Sample Lesson

Step 1:   Ask your students to list different shows that are on television.

Step 2:   Ask students to create classifications for these action, comedy, cartoons, romances, and so on.

Step 3:   Ask students to place the different shows into the different classifications.

Step 4:   Ask students to identify which criteria they used.

Step 5:   Lead a discussion about how they decided on their criteria.

Other peoples' classifications can be used to influence you and your family. For example, ketchup is classified as a vegetable in many school systems. Always ask, "Does this classification make sense and does it serve my clear intentions?"

Step 5:   Ask students to brainstorm different ways that classification is important.

Step 6:   Create a list of all the different ways that classification is important.

Step 7:   On an ongoing basis ask students to identify classification in their everyday lessons.

A Story About Classification

It could have meant a nuclear war between the United States and the Russia. A convoy of ships was heading towards Cuba, some of which were loaded with missiles to be aimed at the United States mainland. President Kennedy had to decide how to handle this deadly situation. He had recently read a book called the Guns of August *that documents the escalation of conflict in world wars. In his mind, he may have created a classification of factors that escalate conflict. The administration then worked diligently to avoid triggering standard rules of engagement, such as firing warning shots across the bows of the approaching ships or returning fire when spy planes were shot at. By classifying this type of action as communication, the administration was able eventually to convince the Russia to agree to remove the missiles from Cuba.*

125

When students make connections
they increase their cognitive schema
and then have more knowledge on
the topic of study.

Cognitive Asset: Making Connections

Our Challenge: "Many students do not make links between classroom and life, or between different content areas. Without links, knowledge can be fragile and fragmented."

Definition: The skill and capacity to make links between different sources of information in a way that creates deeper meaning and understanding.

Teacher Intent: To model and mediate the making of links between different sources of information as a way to create meaning and deepen understanding.

Research suggests that traditional education, in which information is presented and regurgitated without meaningful connections being made, results in low levels of learning. Studies also suggest that, when students create their own connections between what is being learned in the classroom and their own lives, higher academic achievement can follow.

Making Connections: A Sample Lesson

Step 1:   Begin by "hooking" the students with a motivational question or story to introduce the lesson's content.

Step 2:   Ask the students to make connections between the topic of study today and what they already know about it from previous experiences.

Step 3:   Ask if they are surprised to learn how much they already know about this topic of study.

Step 4:   Now, ask what interests them further about the topic.

Step 5:   In the de-briefing after this lesson, ask the students to consider the importance of making connections habitually in study as well as in life.

127

Cultivating the asset of making
meaningful connections is the key to
understanding.

Sample Guiding Questions

What do I *already know* about this topic?
Now what do I *want to learn* about this topic?
How can I *use what I learned* in other situations?

A Story of
Making Connections in Action

We have had the pleasure of knowing many great teachers who are proud of their teaching and learning with students we call courageous learners, those who often struggle with school. Often these teachers of courageous learners tell us of student successes when the learners have an opportunity to connect their problem-solving skills used at home with problem solving at school. These master teachers report that creating the opportunity for these courageous students to share their often clear thinking used outside of school offers a chance for them to learn to use the same cognitive assets at school.

The adage "people who fail
to plan, plan to fail" has a certain
ring of truth. Education systems that
fail to teach students to plan, by
the same token, may be planning
for their students to fail.

♀ Cognitive Asset: Systematic Planning

Our Challenge: "Some students jump into the answer before they even think about planning their response. Others don't even begin!"

Definition: Appropriate planning behavior that is organized in a way that leads to a well-expressed response.

Teacher Intent: To facilitate a need within the student to use an organized method to plan for solving any problem in life and school. As guide, the teacher amplifies the *process* of planning in an organized way.

After students have been introduced to systematic search and have practiced using it (as the first part of the process of problem solving), they are ready to practice planning as the second part of the process. As with all aspects of thinking, give students many chances to develop examples about when the planning phase of problem solving makes the difference between success and failure.

Systematic Planning: A Sample Lesson

Step 1:   Ask the students when in their lives it has been important for them to make a plan in order to succeed at something.

Step 2:   Tell a story of two different families. One family makes a plan for the summer vacation and another does not.

Step 3:   Have the students discuss possible scenarios that could happen with these two families.

Step 4:   Ask the students what a good plan for a vacation includes.

Step 5:   Create a mind map of the class plan as a group.

Step 6:   Discuss what could go wrong if you don't have a good plan.

Step 7:   Plan follow-up lessons that allow the students to be able to plan for success.

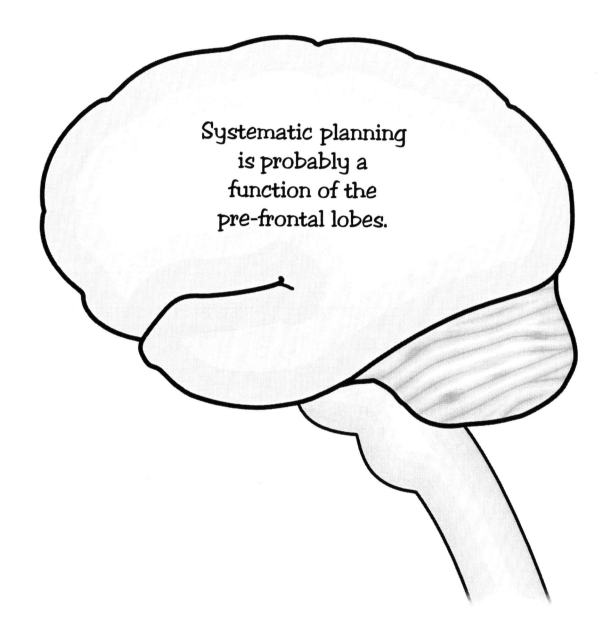

Systematic planning is probably a function of the pre-frontal lobes.

Sample Guiding Questions

What is my plan to solve this problem?
Have I *mapped out my plan* so I will have a visual of it?
Do I *have what I need* to implement the plan?

Learning to Make a Plan:
A Story Told Happily By Mother

After lessons such as these in gathering information and using it to make a good plan, many students we have taught tell stories of their use of these thinking blocks at home and school. Here is one parent's recollection of her daughter's journey to becoming a better problem solver while experiencing Donna's coaching for learning in Sue's elementary school. Sue's parents were both very glad that the school offered classes in thinking where the knowledge and skills could be used at home as well as at school. Before she began to develop a systematic approach to problem solving and other thinking skills, Sue had great difficulty with schoolwork.

Sue:	*"Dad, you can do better if you use systematic planning. It will help you organize your desk better."*
Father:	*"I need to what? Hey, Mom, what in the world is Susie talking about?"*
Mother:	*"I didn't hear her. What did you say, Sue?"*
Sue:	*"I told Dad he should use systematic planning to help him get better organized."*
Father:	*"Where is she learning these skills and vocabulary?"*
Mother:	*"At school. Her teacher and others have begun using a learning to learn approach. They are planning to hold a meeting soon to see if parents want to join them by helping our children learn to learn at home."*
Sue:	*"In my class we're building a learning community and using building blocks and tools for thinking to make strategies so we don't have trouble learning."*
Mother:	*"So... what did you tell Dad?"*
Sue:	*"I just told him that if he uses systematic planning he will be able to decide on a strategy for organizing his stuff. Maybe he needs self-regulation, too!"*

133

Cognitive flexibility makes a difference for the better in student performance on tests; in adult marriages; and on the job.

💡 Cognitive Asset: Cognitive Flexibility

Our Challenge: "The era of high stakes testing and higher standards for student achievement has created an environment where flexible thinking is critical to academic success. For example, many test questions are designed to deliberately cause students to use familiar thinking patterns that may result in a wrong answer."

Definition: The skill and capacity for accurately assessing situations and adjusting thoughts and actions appropriately.

Teacher Intent: To demonstrate and mediate the benefits of flexible thinking as a means to solve problems and achieve goals.

Some have said that the skill of men and women to shift roles into a cooperative family member after a hard day's work is one of the most predictive elements of a marriage. Take, for example, the spouse who cannot quit talking about the colleague at work that he or she cannot get along with. The mate in our example will surely be seen as being angry and boring by their husband or wife as they continuously speak of work and focus on their own dislikes. The spouse, however, who is cognitively flexible and can shift from a career-oriented or job-focused state to being a mate who is interested in home events, will be much appreciated.

Teachers also report the great importance of cognitive flexibility for student success. What teacher has not said to their mathematics students, "Pay attention to the operational sign in math problems. The signs often change, and when you continue with the same operation when it changes from problem to problem, you will have many points subtracted on daily work and tests."

Cognitive Flexibility: A Sample Lesson

Step 1:   First introduce the term cognitive flexibility to your students.

Step 2:   Next read the following script to the students.

Script

Erin rose to hear her parents arguing downstairs. She covered her head and thought, "I wish they would stop, just for one morning." She looked in the bathroom mirror only to look into a very tired face. Nothing unusual for Erin, for she always stays up late arguing with

135

Einstein is credited with saying that a definition of insanity is to keep doing what isn't working and expecting different results.

her little brother, and ends up getting less than enough sleep. Then Erin had a positive thought. She remembered that she had received good marks on her paper the day before when her favorite teacher noticed that she had put forth a lot of effort on an important paper. "Maybe," thought Erin this morning, I can make this a better day than usual after all.

Step 3: Ask your students how Erin can use cognitive flexibility to help her create a better than usual day for herself.

Step 4: Ask the students to reflect and discover when it has been necessary for them to use this important asset in their lives before.

Step 5: Ask them when they plan to use this asset next.

Sample Guiding Questions

Is what I am currently thinking and doing *working well*?
What are my *cues* that things are going well, or not? How do I check?
If things are not going as well as they can,
then what do I need to think and do *differently*?

A Story of
Cognitive Flexibility in Action

If you are a teacher, how many times have you started a day with a plan for your teaching in mind, only to find that 10 minutes after starting you must be somewhat flexible in the implementation of your plan? For example, a BrainSMART graduate student and master teacher had an effective plan in mind to teach the very important cognitive asset of systematic planning. As she drove to school she thought of the power of this cognitive asset to transform lives for the better. She got to school and when it was time for lessons to began, she threw out her motivational hook and the students were off and running with the lesson. Just as the students were standing up a few minutes into the lesson, the fire alarm went off and all had to leave the building. The teacher's cognitive flexibility was tested! Thirty minutes later, the fire drill over, the teacher and students were back in the room, and the teacher excitedly resumed her important lesson.

137

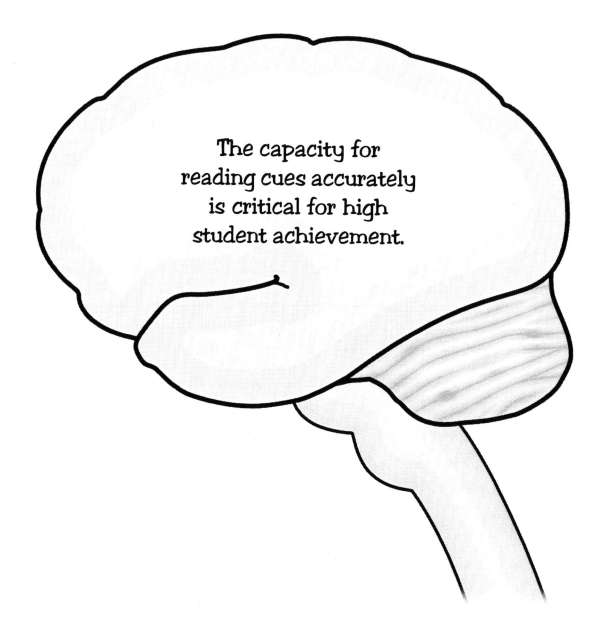

The capacity for
reading cues accurately
is critical for high
student achievement.

💡 Cognitive Asset: Using Cues Appropriately

Our Challenge: "My students do not seem to know what is important to consider in problem solving. They often miss important verbal and nonverbal cues."

Definition: The ability to use necessary information given in the world to solve academic and life problems.

Teacher Intent: To guide students to seek out necessary verbal and non-verbal information (and also to know what is not necessary) in order to solve problems.

Do you have students who do not search for the necessary and relevant cues to use to solve problems? There are two major difficulties that we have seen over and over with this asset. One error is that the students attempt to use too much information, including that which is irrelevant. The other error is made when they overlook too much information and, thus, do not consider the important and necessary information.

Using Cues Appropriately: A Sample Lesson

Step 1:   Begin any academic task. For example, begin a mathematics reading problem such as the following:

The average person needs about 2000 calories a day to stay healthy and active. In the United States, 3800 calories a day (per person) worth of food and drink is produced. A lot of people like pizza and ice cream. How many calories per day per person are surplus to the average person's needs?

Step 2:   Tell the students that your clear intent is that they will solve the problem correctly by using the cognitive asset of using cues appropriately.

Step 3:   Ask the students, "What information is available in this problem?"

Step 4:   Ask the students, "What information of what is given is needed to solve this problem?"

139

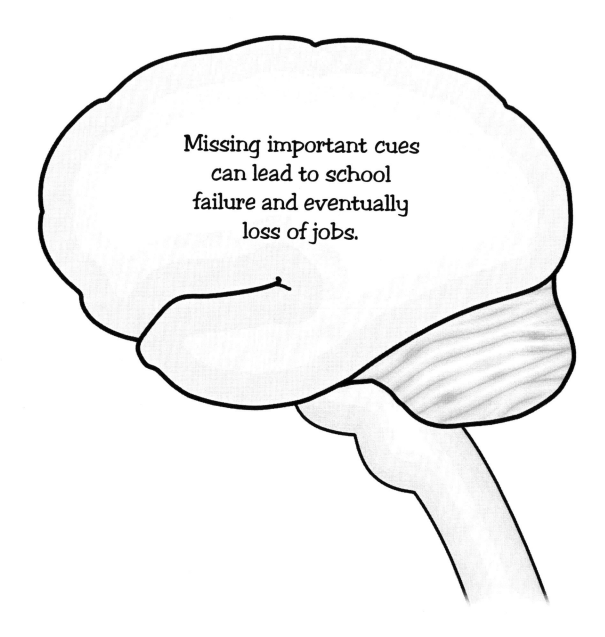

Missing important cues
can lead to school
failure and eventually
loss of jobs.

Step 5:   Then ask the students, "Name the information that is given but not necessary."

Step 6:   Ask the students solve the problem using the necessary cues.

Step 7:   After the students solve the problem, ask for volunteers to work through the process focusing on using cues appropriately.

Step 8:   When the problem is solved correctly, to aid transfer, ask the students "When in life do we need to use our ability to use cues appropriately?" Or, an example could be more specific: "When we are looking for a friend, what cues indicate that a person might be a good friend?"

Step 9:   After the above discussion, ask when else in academics do we need to use cues appropriately? For example, we might ask, "When do we need to use cues appropriately in test taking?"

A Story About Using Cues Appropriately

In a BrainSMART workshop we were teaching the cognitive asset of using cues appropriately, a participant suddenly burst out with an Ah-ha! He said do you know that I never actually thought of this as an important aspect of life, but now I see how it is. I think that by not using this asset and never having a father to help me learn it, I have lost some jobs due to inappropriate behavior. I have also lost girlfriends due to the fact that I did not read their cues appropriately about how I might befriend them. Now I know how to use this, and I think it will change me. I want to teach this to at-risk students as I do not think many of them have this skill of using cues appropriately!

141

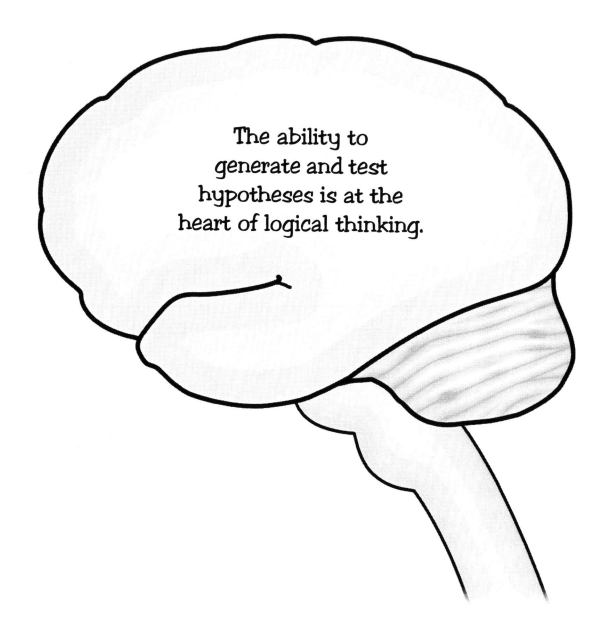

The ability to
generate and test
hypotheses is at the
heart of logical thinking.

🛈 Cognitive Asset: Making Inferences/Hypothetical Thinking

Our Challenge: "My students do not think beyond given information. On problems where they have to think themselves, they often do not know how and miss problems on tests as a result."

Definition: The ability to solve problems and create new information by making inferences based on the information given. To go beyond what is said to a logical conclusion that is not explicitly given.

Teacher Intent: To create within students the understanding of the importance of making correct inferences and thinking beyond the given in a logical manner.

Making Inferences/Hypothetical Thinking: A Sample Lesson

This lesson plan is designed to be used in the context of teaching reading.

Step 1: Ask students to choose a reading assignment that will help them practice making inferences and generating hypotheses.

Step 2: Look closely at the title of the reading assignment.

Step 3: Generate a hypothesis about the content of this reading based on the information given in the title and on the book cover.

Step 4: Highlight three passages from the reading assignment you consider to be most important.

Step 5: What inferences can be made from each of these key passages? In other words, what is logical to infer from each of the passages about the reading?

Step 6: Having read the reading assignment, revisit your hypothesis (Step 3) about the reading. Was your hypothesis correct or incorrect? If correct, what were your cues that lead to a correct hypothesis? If incorrect, what cues were missed?

143

In any context the cognitive
asset of making good inferences
is key to performance. For example,
Wall Street traders who correctly create
inferences of market movements
earn millions of dollars.

Step 7: Now revisit your inferences from Step 5. Were they correct or incorrect? If correct, what were your cues that guided you to your inference? If incorrect, what did you miss?

Step 8: What have you learned in this lesson about your problem solving?

Summary

So many students we've met have the skill to make inferences, but do not realize what this cognitive asset is and how they can use it to their advantage at school. As they explicitly learn more about this asset, it makes a great difference in their lives.

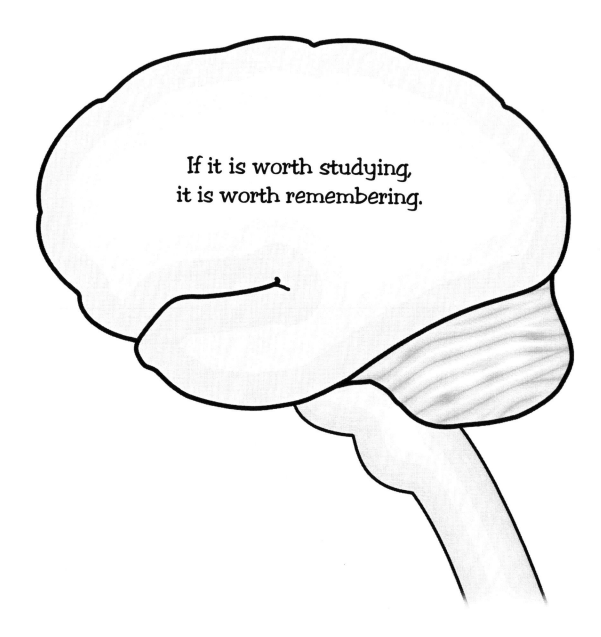

If it is worth studying,
it is worth remembering.

♀ Cognitive Asset: Working Memory

Our Challenge: "We are getting more and more students who keep nodding their heads while we are teaching as if they really learning, then three days later they forget everything."

Definition: The skill of consciously choosing what to retain in long-term memory, and selecting appropriate tools to retain and recall information to achieve desired results.

Teacher Intent: To facilitate student's skills in identifying what information is important to retain, and in choosing effective memory tools.

One of the critical cognitive assets for increasing academic achievement is working memory. Many students can work hard to load learning into their brains, but when they sit down to take a test their minds go blank. They cannot access and apply what they have learned. A powerful way to enhance students' feeling of competence is to teach them tools of working memory and for them to experience the thrill of organizing information in way that they can recall it and succeed during tests and in life.

Working Memory: A Sample Lesson

Step 1: Explain to your students that their brain saves and deletes information like a computer.

Step 2: Ask students when is it important to save information.

Step 3: Ask students if they have ever hit "delete" when they take tests.

Step 4: Teach students to use some of the memory tools from *BrainSMART Strategies for Boosting Test Scores* (2000).

Step 5: Give students some key information to load into working memory. Guide them into using an appropriate tool.

Step 6: Let students "show off" their success.

Step 7: Ask students to describe how it feels to make their memory work well.

147

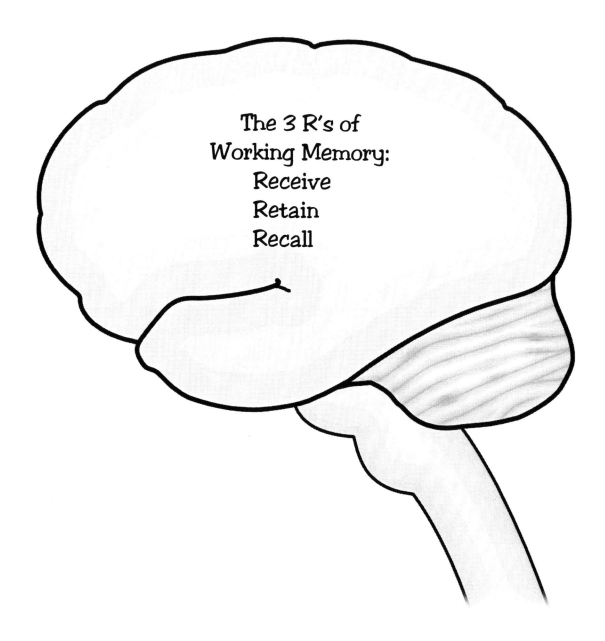

The 3 R's of
Working Memory:
Receive
Retain
Recall

Sample Guiding Questions

What do I really need to *store* in my working memory?
What might be the *most effective* memory tools for the task?
How can I *strengthen* my working memory through practice?

A Story of Working Memory in the Classroom

Donna was working in the classroom with a large group of students as part of a state-wide initiative. All the students had been identified as having learning difficulties. She taught them several tools for boosting working memory and used complex information about the brain as her subject matter. Then she gave them a test in front of the principal, a visiting Teacher of the Year, and journalists from two newspapers. The students all answered virtually 100% right. There was a huge celebration. How long do you think they will remember that day?

149

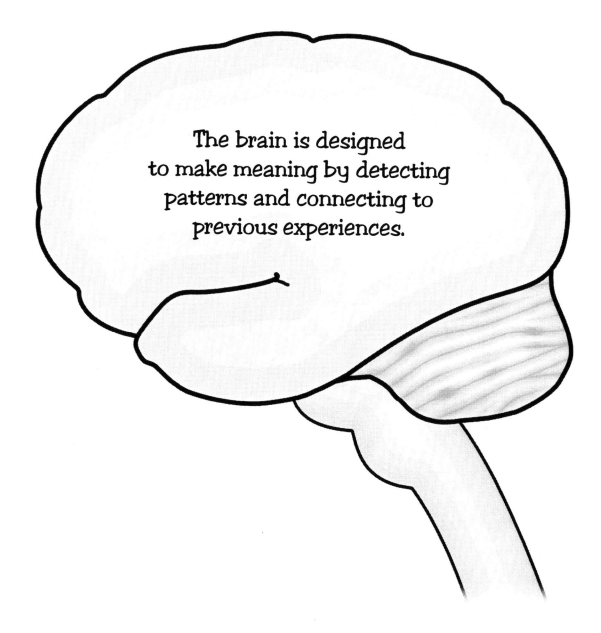

The brain is designed
to make meaning by detecting
patterns and connecting to
previous experiences.

💡 Cognitive Asset: Making Meaning

Challenge: "My students do not seem to be interested in the curriculum we are teaching here. It seems meaningless to them."

Definition: The ability to access past experiences, connect with the new, and infuse an appropriate amount of energy into the learning experience knowing that it is important to life.

Teacher Intent: To teach lessons that have great meaning in an energized way that helps students develop curiosity about the topic of study. To ask questions that will help students connect new information in working memory with that in long-term schema.

What is it that you love and love to study about? We hope this is the content and process that you are teaching! The cognitive asset of making meaning is about helping students learn to develop their own meaning in life through our valuing and energizing what we teach with them. There has been debate about values in education. However, given that there is now evidence that emotions and thought are connected, it is important that we help students give life, energy, and meaning to material that we ask them to think about.

Making Meaning: A Sample Lesson

The lesson is to help students learn to make meaning from a lecture.

Step 1:   Tell the students, "Clear your mind of all distractions."

Step 2:   Identify how this lecture can have personal meaning in terms of moving them towards their goals.

Step 3:   Ask them to predict what they will learn in this lecture.

Step 4:   As they make notes or make a mind map (or brain web), ask them to focus on two factors: factor 1, the content of the lecture and factor 2, how the content of the lecture links to your personal or academic life.

Step 5:   Remind them that, when appropriate, they may ask questions of the lecturer that helps them understand the material.

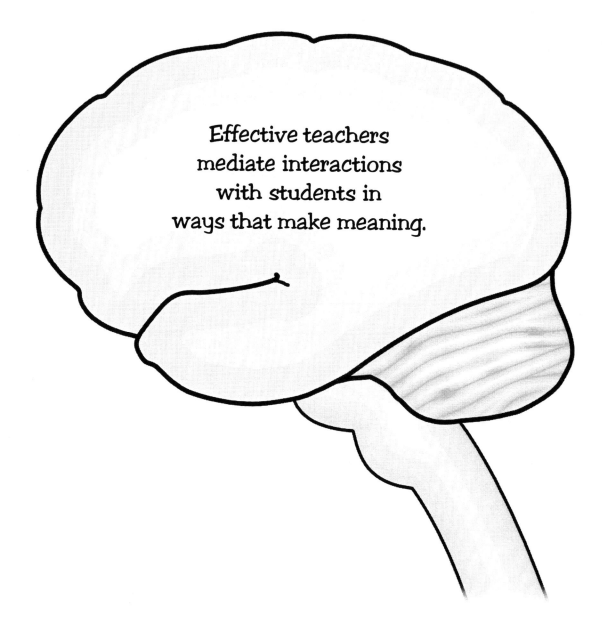

Effective teachers
mediate interactions
with students in
ways that make meaning.

Step 6: After the lecture, ask them to review their notes carefully and notice what is particularly meaningful and important to them.

Step 7: Tell them to recreate the essence of the lecture using pictures, metaphors, and stories that illustrate the key points, and present to a friend.

Step 8: Have them actively seek links between what they learned in a lecture and what they read elsewhere or saw on television or in their everyday life.

A Story about Making Meaning

At a BrainSMART workshop in Texas, a group of students were asked what they had learned from the experience. The topic of study was becoming metacognitive, and (in this case) we had taught strategies for remembering information. One student replied thoughtfully, "From now on I'm gonna be the boss of my brain. I know I can!"

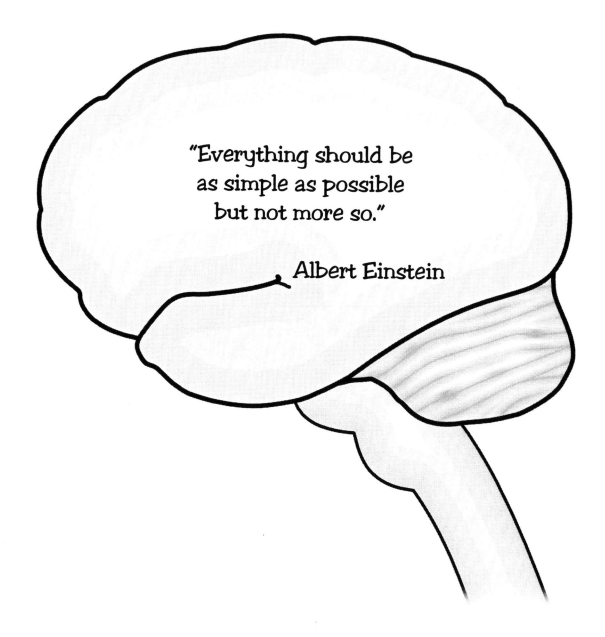

"Everything should be as simple as possible but not more so."

Albert Einstein

💡 Cognitive Asset: Summarizing

Our Challenge: "I have students who do not know how to identify what is important, what is irrelevant, or to summarize what is important in a succinct way."

Definition: The behavior of identifying what is most salient and important and communicating it in verbal or written form succinctly.

Teacher Intent: To cultivate in students the ability to identify what is most important, and how to summarize their communication of this in verbal and written modalities.

One of the most powerful ways to communicate clearly so that the message is received and understood is to summarize content in a succinct verbal or written message. Research by Miller suggested that the human brain can process 5 to 9 units information at a time. For example, most phone numbers are seven digits. When the authors teach students and teachers about the human brain and attention, they use the metaphor of the octopus with eight tentacles ready to juggle information as it is received by the conscious mind. Now imagine what happens when that octopus is thrown 50 pieces of information without knowing what is most important. When your brain is listening to somebody speak who does not summarize well, it may well hit overload and delete the intended meaning of the communication.

An area of the brain known as the hippocampus and shaped like a seahorse is involved in the process of moving information from short-term attention to long-term memory. Some researchers believe that if this area is overloaded with information, it is difficult to process and store information in the cortex.

"Everything should be as simple as possible but not more so."

Albert Einstein

Summarizing: A Sample Lesson

Step 1:   Ask your students if they have any friends or relatives who talk a lot but never summarize and reach a conclusion.

155

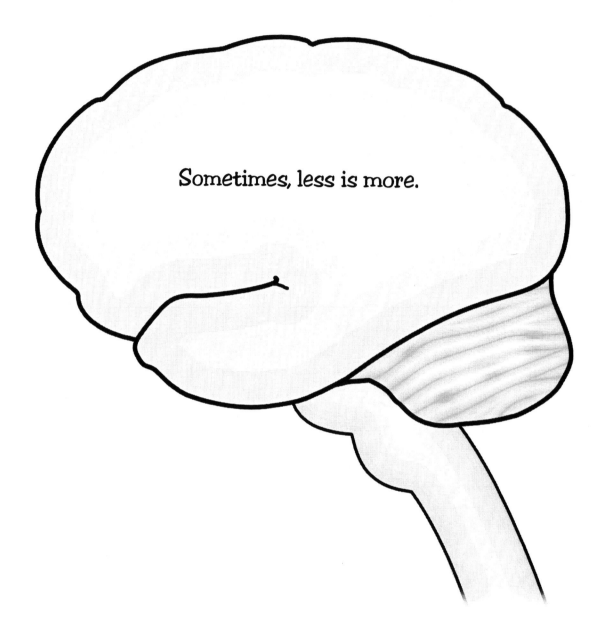

Sometimes, less is more.

Step 2: Ask students to read the two scripts. Or read them aloud.

Script 1:

You know I read this book, you know and it was like so you know, like interesting. There was this guy who wanted to join the circus and become a clown. I think clowns are scary and I wonder why they have those big shoes. My cousin has big shoes he likes pizza. I like pizza too. Specially with lots of vegetables like broccoli. Anyway this guy went to Los Angeles for an interview and he tried to get a train. I got a train once and it was late. There was a cool lady on the train who had a blue dress on and a white straw hat and she kept "saying I'm going to be late I'm going to be late." So this guy wants to get on the train so the he can get to the interview but he misses the train and gets mad. I get mad sometimes when my brother picks on me. It's not fair. What was I talking about again?

Script 2:

I read this book about a man who wanted to become a clown. He tried to get to an interview, but he missed the train.

Step 3: Ask your students to identify what was different about each script.

Step 4: Ask your students to identify the benefits of summarizing.

Step 5: Ask your students to identify the benefits of not summarizing.

Step 6.: Ask your students to identify times when summarizing would be a useful asset.

Sample Guiding Questions

What is *most important* in what I want to communicate?
What are the *who, what, where, how, why,* and *when* in the message?
How can I *reduce what I want to communicate* to the shortest
number of words?

Communication is
the problem of getting
ideas from
one brain to another.

Chapter 8

Output:
Making It Real
(Communication)

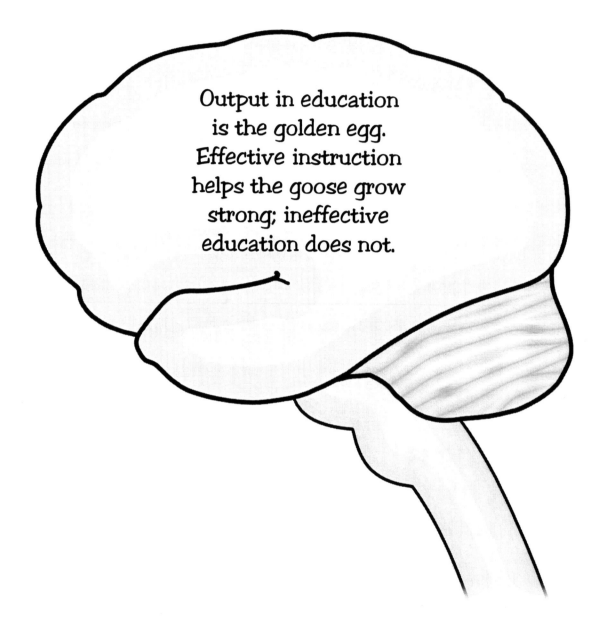

Output in education
is the golden egg.
Effective instruction
helps the goose grow
strong; ineffective
education does not.

Introduction

The third phase of genius in our model represents the movement from potential to word and action in the world. It is, if you will, the payoff phase. To a physician who has gathered information and diagnosed the problem, the output phase is when they prescribe appropriate treatment. To a student in the classroom, it is the phase when, after gathering information from many sources and processing the information to make meaning from it, they create the assigned essay. In education systems today, student achievement test scores are based essentially on student output. Therefore, the cognitive assets in this output phase are critical to supporting school and life success.

Often, when students are having difficulty at school, they need a strong dose of coaching at the input and output phases. Less often, intervention is needed at the processing phase.

Many students who need coaching at the output phase benefit from work at the input and processing levels as well. To illustrate, consider the student who exhibits very impulsive and non-systematic behavior at the input level. Perhaps this same student also rarely shows evidence of considering another person's point of view at the output level. On the other hand, some who need coaching in the output phase only need work in the third phase of genius. For example, think of the student who seems to have a full complement of cognitive assets in place in most situations, but rarely uses the asset of finishing power. This is the usually smart functioning student, curious and with many ideas, who perhaps ends up making low grades at school because he or she rarely uses the cognitive asset of finishing power.

Although districts and schools across the United States are mainly focused on the products of education, primarily test scores and grades, we believe that the way to achieve success in school and life is through systematic use of the cognitive assets within the three-phase model. Furthermore, although these products are important, we believe that it is also critical that other aspects of output are key to performance as well. Consider the output assets described in the following examples.

Appropriate Courage—Example 1

One critical asset for achieving success in school and in life is that of appropriate courage. Individuals who have cultivated this cognitive asset are good at calculating the costs and benefits of important decisions and actions. For example, research suggests that teachers with a positive self-concept are six times more likely to learn and transfer new knowledge and best practice to the classroom. They have the appropriate courage to take a small risk in hopes

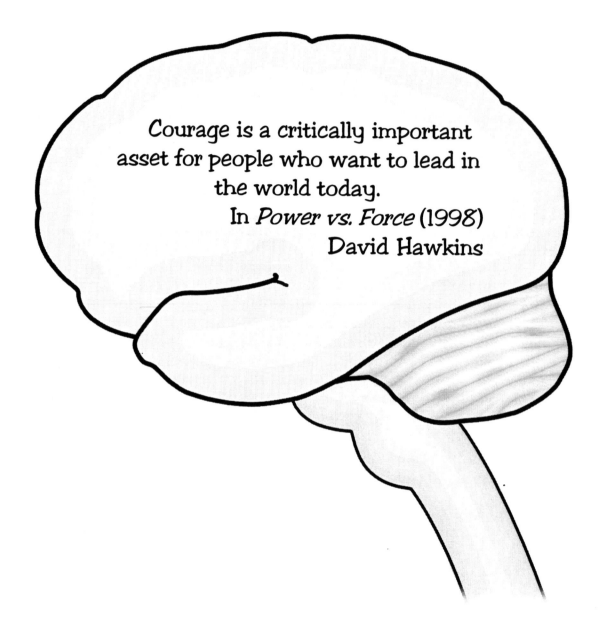

Courage is a critically important asset for people who want to lead in the world today.
In *Power vs. Force* (1998)
David Hawkins

of a large reward of greater personal satisfaction and increased student learning among their students. Students who have failed in mathematics again and again and yet still arrive in mathematics class are exhibiting appropriate courage to try to learn mathematics once more.

Finishing Power—Example 2

The 21st century is a time when individuals and organizations are increasingly judged by the value that they deliver. Many people are great at starting projects and talking about ideas or a better way of doing things. This, of course, creates the potential for delivering value. However, it is only when ideas become real in the world through action that the value is realized. For example, there was a television commercial that stated, "It's not how many ideas you have that is important; it's how many ideas that are implemented that counts." We have been so impressed with teachers who have attended our workshops or attended graduate studies; gathered ideas; and then demonstrated the cognitive asset of finishing power to translate research-based ideas into practical applications that work in their classrooms.

Learning from Experience—Example 3

It is said that people who fail to learn from history are destined to repeat the same mistakes. Many of us make the same mistakes over and over again because we fail to learn from our experience. For example, some educators have 20 years of experience in which they have thoughtfully reflected upon and constantly improved their practice, whereas other educators simply repeated one year of experience 20 times. In most successful organizations, a specific process of learning from experience is considered critical to survival and success.

For example, the U.S. military invests millions of dollars in what they call the after action review process. In the after action review, representatives from all ranks give candid feedback as to what happened in a recent exercise or combat situation. In short, the cognitive asset of learning from experience may be described as a part of the process of acquiring wisdom.

Output Phase: Six Cognitive Assets

Cognitive Assets: Point of View

Challenge: "I have students who are often in trouble because they can not see from anybody else's point of view. This makes it hard for them to enjoy reading or to understand new ways of looking at things."

Definition: Appropriate understanding and respect for other people's point of view that manifests itself in empathy and rapport.

Teacher Intent: To facilitate the need within the student to be curious about how others see the world. As guide, the teacher amplifies the process of gathering information and deepening understanding of different viewpoints.

One of the most difficult cognitive assets to cultivate is to understand and respect the point of view of others. Most of us are content to make quick judgments about other people and have little curiosity about different ways of seeing the world. It is easy to get in a rut of knowing we are right, and the rest of the world is wrong. It is easy to stick with people who have the same views as we do and who do not challenge us to look beyond the superficial. In our relationships with people of the opposite gender, for example, it is difficult to understand why they see the world the way they do. This may explain why some researchers find that 67% of first marriages end in divorce (Gottman & Silver, 1999). It may also explain why effective teachers work hard at understanding the point of view of their students. This may also explain why peer mediation works so well. The authors like to use the 6/9 cartoon in workshops to help people to consider the point of view of others.

Point of View: A Sample Lesson

Step 1: Ask your students to think about a time when they did not feel understood. You might wish to think of an example from your own life.

Step 2: Show the cartoon to your students.

Step 3: Ask them to articulate what they see.

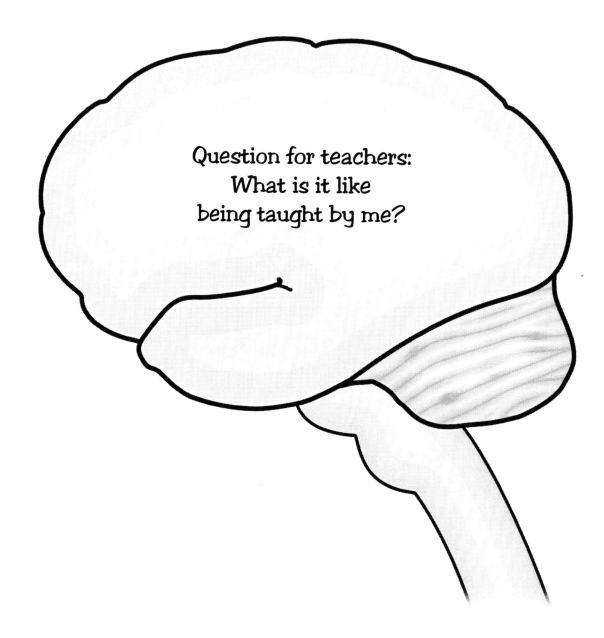

Question for teachers:
What is it like
being taught by me?

Step 4: Ask them to explain what would be a good way to see from the others point of view.

Step 5: Ask students to think of think of times when they have not seen the world from another's point of view.

Sample Guiding Questions

What is the *other person seeing* from where they are?
Ask the *question* "Why do you say that?"
What would it look, feel, and sound like *if I was in their shoes?*

"The test of a first rate intelligence is the ability to hold two opposed ideas in the mind at the same time and still retain the ability to function."

F. Scott Fitzgerald

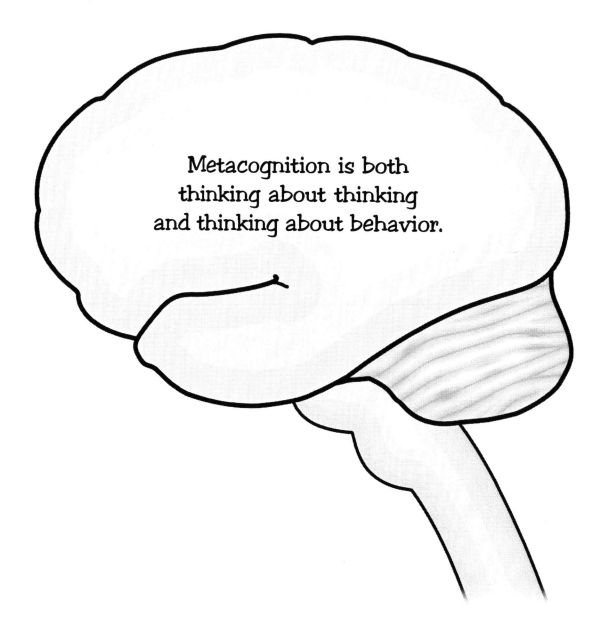

Metacognition is both
thinking about thinking
and thinking about behavior.

💡 Cognitive Asset: Thoughtful Behavior

Challenge: "My students do not think before they respond. Their answers are often not well thought out. They need to stop and think and not be so impulsive."

Definition: The ability to stop, think, and respond in a manner that is appropriate in the situation.

Teacher Intent: To guide students to develop the ability to reflect appropriately before responding. This asset can only be used after the students have been taught to search systematically and process information before responding in a thoughtful way at the output level.

Thoughtful Behavior: A Sample Lesson

This lesson could be used in most any situation.

Step 1:   Ask yourself the W.I.N. question, "What's important now?"

Step 2:   Having identified "What's important now?" ask, "What's happening now?"

Step 3:   Ask the question, "What is not happening now?"

Step 4:   Ask the question, "How can my current behavior or communication influence the situation?"

Step 5:   How can I change my behavior (or communication) to increase the probability that I will achieve a step toward "What's important now?"

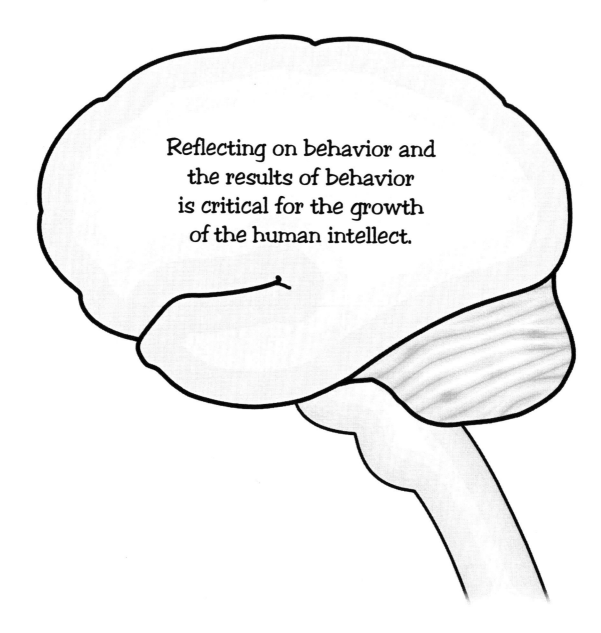

Reflecting on behavior and
the results of behavior
is critical for the growth
of the human intellect.

A Story About Thoughtful Behavior

In a classroom in Port St. Lucie, Florida, we recently observed a third-grade student recalling names of the planets. Her BrainSMART teacher gave her plenty of time to reflect and use the strategy of association to remember the planets. She was very thoughtful for about 4 minutes as she accessed the information and, when she completed the task, she answered correctly. No one in the class interrupted her. This teacher is fostering active reflection that results in thoughtful behavior.

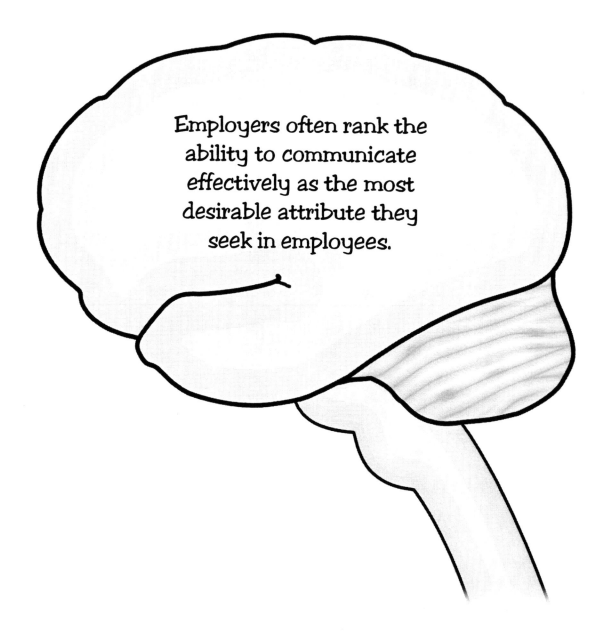

Employers often rank the ability to communicate effectively as the most desirable attribute they seek in employees.

ⓦ Cognitive Asset: Effective Expression

Challenge: "The answers some of our students give! It is as if they just give the first one off the top of their heads!"

Definition: A thoughtful response made after adequate exploration and planning is completed.

Teacher Intent: To facilitate a need within the student to communicate in a way that will help them be successful at school and in life. As guide, the teacher amplifies the *process* of effective expression.

When students understand and use systematic search and effective planning, they are ready to discuss and use controlled self-expression. As they add the third phase of problem solving to their practice, continue to question the students about the need for the first two phases so that they understand systematic search, planning, and self-expression as a connected process.

Effective Expression: A Sample Lesson

Step 1: State to the whole class, "Today as we take a test I would like for you to be aware of your outlook."

Step 2: Ask them to remember the discussions and exercises for creating an optimistic outlook.

Step 3: Remind them that as they work on the test to remember to breathe deeply when necessary and to recall that they are in their "Success Seats." For more on the Success Seat Tool see BrainSMART Strategies for Boosting Test Scores (2000).

Step 4: Discuss the importance of using controlled self-expression even when it is difficult.

Sample Guiding Questions

Am I being impulsive in answering this question?
Have I *considered others' point of view* before making my response?
Have I *rehearsed my response* so that I won't get
emotionally blocked when I speak?
Did I *edit my paper* before turning it in?

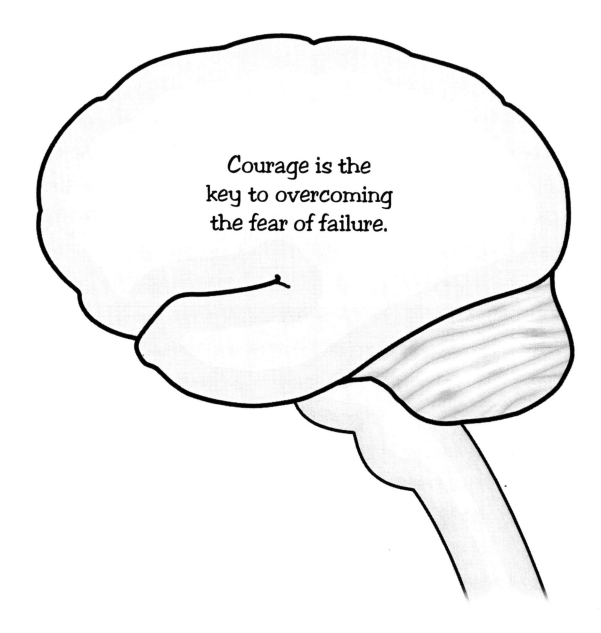

Courage is the
key to overcoming
the fear of failure.

💡 Cognitive Asset: Appropriate Courage

Challenge: "We have, in our classrooms, some students who seem to fearful to contribute to their lessons in learning. At the other extreme, we have other students who blurt things out impulsively and get themselves into trouble."

Definition: Appropriate courage is the cognitive asset of assessing situations, being clear on mission and goals, and taking appropriate action.

Teacher Intent To model and coach appropriate courage in everyday instructional practice. For example, letting students know you have learned a new strategy and that you want to try it out in the classroom.

Appropriate courage is the cognitive asset that brings risk assessment, motivation, and clear intent into immediate action. For example, some students are extremely risk averse when it comes to learning or trying something new. This will manifest itself in deflecting behavior aversions, such as asking a lot of questions when they know the answers; saying they can not find resources like pen, paper, or book; or saying that they have already done it! At the other end of the continuum, we see students engaging in highly risky behavior without being aware of the risks, such as experimenting with drugs.

Appropriate courage involves accurately assessing a situation and the inherent risks, being clear on mission or goals, deciding what action to take, being clear about what resources are needed, and what an appropriate timeline is. This is, in essence, making SMART decisions and following through even when it is scary. The truth is that staying too long in our comfort zone can atrophy our muscles for appropriate courage. For example, research suggests that confident competent educators are much more likely to try new strategies in the classroom (Moye, 1997). This in turn increases the probability that they will be more effective more of the time with more students, which, in turn, increases their capacity for appropriate courage. Less confident teachers tend to be less likely to try new ideas and to give up sooner, thereby, reducing their chances of success. One way to cultivate appropriate courage is to focus on a clear set of questions when an opportunity presents itself.

175

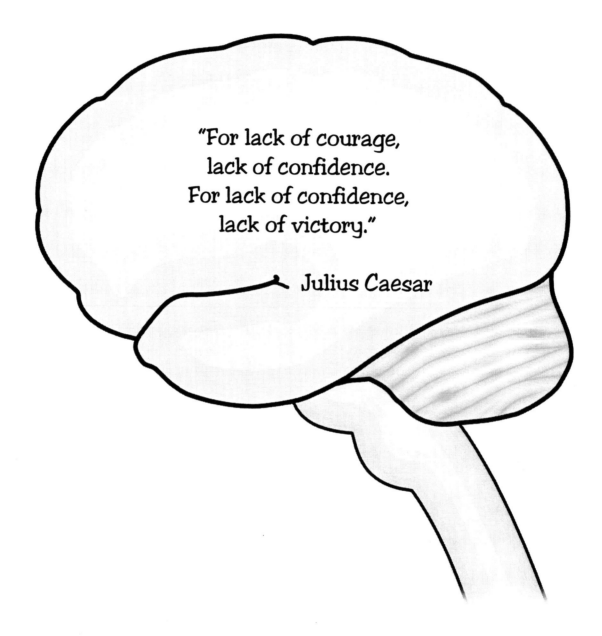

"For lack of courage,
lack of confidence.
For lack of confidence,
lack of victory."

Julius Caesar

Sample Plan — SMART

Step 1:   S —   What is the Situation? What are the risks or rewards possible in this situation?

Step 2:   M —   What is my Mission or goal? Will this really help me reach my goals?

Step 3:   A —   What Action is appropriate? What is an effective next step?

Step 4:   R —   What Resources do I need to be successful?

Step 5:   T —   What is a realistic Timeline? How long will it take? How much time should I invest?

Sample Guiding Questions:
The Three R's of Appropriate Courage

What *Results* do I want?
What are the *Rewards* of this opportunity?
What are the *Risks* involved in this opportunity?

Possible Examples of
Appropriate Courage for Educators

1. Sitting in the front row during professional development.
2. Trying out new strategies with your students.
3. Admitting mistakes.
4. Speaking up in faculty meetings when you feel strongly.
5. Saying no when appropriate.

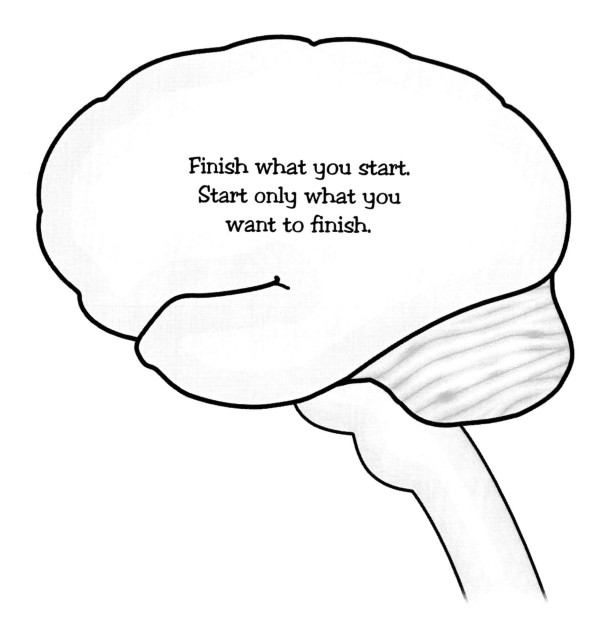

Finish what you start.
Start only what you
want to finish.

⚡ Cognitive Asset: Finishing Power

Our Challenge: " Some students never seem to finish important tasks. They have great energy to start new tasks, but lose steam fast when it gets difficult or too dull to sustain interest."

Definition: Appropriate task completion behavior that is sustained over time and in spite of difficulty.

Teacher Intent: To cultivate the asset of finishing power by modeling a commitment to completing important tasks in the face of difficulty. To facilitate a need in the student to keep going until a task is done and to encourage rituals of celebration that build a long term sense of pride in work.

Success in life may be defined, in part, as consistently completing important tasks. This is part of life that is under the control of all of us. It is a cognitive asset that brings all the others to fruition. It may be likened to the vital last part of a bridge that transfers potential to results. Those individuals who cultivate this asset excel often in life because they are reliable and consistently perform well. At the other end of the spectrum are those individuals who have not cultivated this asset. They tend to start many projects with enormous energy and commitment, and then gradually their enthusiasm wanes. They then abandon the project and start another.

Finishing Power: A Sample Lesson

Step 1: Ask students when in their lives it is important for them to consistently complete important tasks.

Step 2: Tell students a story of two different students you have taught: One who finishes important tasks and one who does not.

Step 3: Have students discuss possible scenarios that could happen for these two students.

Step 4: Ask students what a good plan for finishing important tasks looks like.

Step 5: Ask students for an example of a person from history who showed great finishing power, and one who did not.

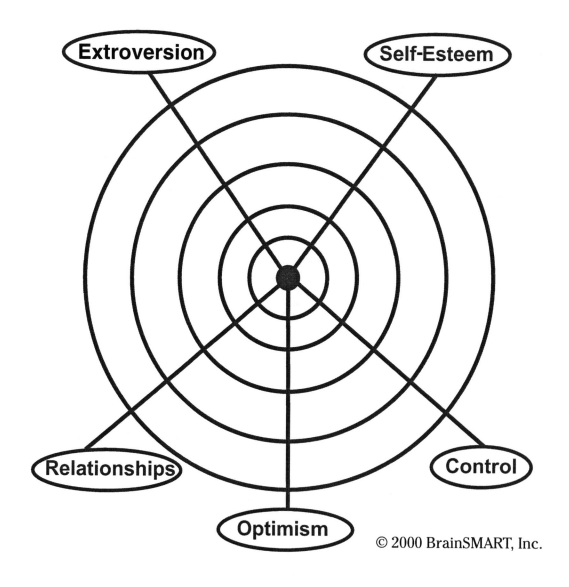

© 2000 BrainSMART, Inc.

Step 6: Create a follow-up lesson plan that allows students to practice and increase their finishing power.

Sample Guiding Questions

Why is important to me that I *complete* this task?
What will it feel like when I *celebrate* completing this task?
What are the *obstacles* I need to overcome to complete this task?
When is the *best time* to get this task completed?
What are the *simple steps* I need to take to complete this task?

Building Finishing Power by Using a WIN WEB

One of the reasons that many people do not finish important tasks is that they do not use motivating visual auditory and kinesthetic cues. See the WIN WEB opposite that Marcus uses everyday to build the cognitive asset of finishing power.

Step 1: List your most important tasks.

Step 2: Write your important tasks into the bubbles on the outside of the WinWeb.

Step 3: Use the WIN WEB to track your progress on your various tasks.

Step 4: Draw a dot as you move closer to finishing the task.

Step 5: When you finish a task, put a dot in the bulls-eye, do an I FEEL GOOD YES, and put a big check mark on the bubble.

Step 6: At the end of the day, review the tasks you have completed and celebrate!

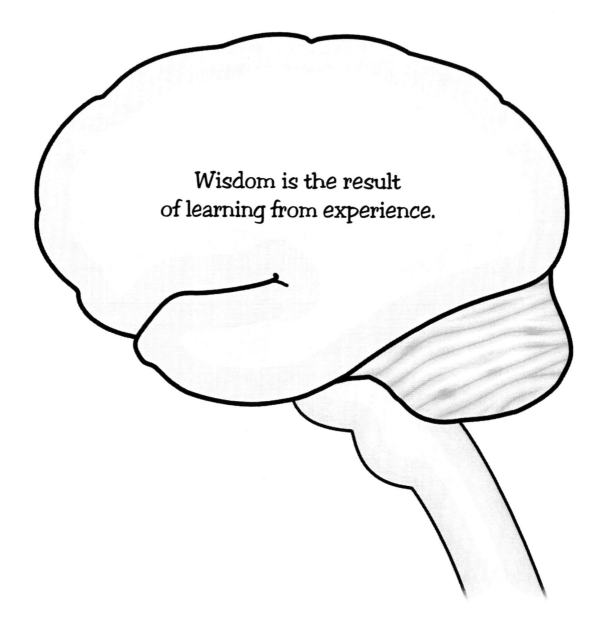

Wisdom is the result
of learning from experience.

🔆 Cognitive Asset: Learning from Experience.

Our Challenge: "We have students who seem to keep making the same mistakes over and over again. They do not seem to learn from their mistakes."

Definition: The skill of reflecting on experience and selecting what to do in the same way or differently the next time.

Teacher Intent: To model "learn from experience" aloud and mediate the cognitive asset of learning from experience.

It is said that wisdom flows not from what happens to us, but what we learn from what happens to us. Many of us keep making the same mistakes over and over again. We spell the same words incorrectly. We lose the same items such as keys and sunglasses. We have all known people who say, "I never want to have a relationship with someone like that again." Weeks later, we see that person with somebody who is a carbon copy of the sort person they did not want be with. The great news is that we can cultivate the asset of learning from experience so that we can turn past failures into resources for getting it right the next time. The overarching resource for learning from experience is metacognition. That is, thinking about our thoughts and actions with a mind towards change when it is necessary.

Learning from Experiences: A Sample Lesson

Step 1:   Ask your students to think of a mistake they often make.

Step 2:   Ask your students how often they make this mistake.

Step 3:   Ask your students to make a plan for avoiding this mistake.

Step 4:   Ask your students to rehearse this in their mind's eye.

Step 5:   Ask your students to notice mistakes they make and reflect on how to avoid them in the future.

Step 6:   Ask your students to notice what goes well in life and to remember to hit the metaphorical *save* key in their minds.

Step 7:   Ask your student to practice reflection and rehearsal at the end of each day.

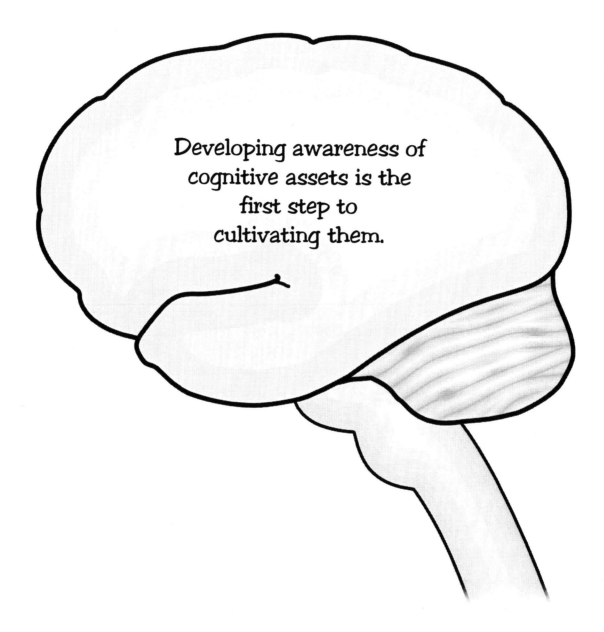

Developing awareness of
cognitive assets is the
first step to
cultivating them.

Summary - All Three Phases and the Cognitive Assets Within the Phases

Now that you have learned about the three phases of genius model, we think that you may view the world of behavior with new eyes! We have enjoyed hearing from educators who have explored and used the model with us. They tell us of stories of how they now see the behavior of their students so much more clearly. Many of them add that, in fact, they also are exploring their own behavior in light of the assets as well. In many of their stories, their appropriate courage to honestly and earnestly make the effort to apply the model has indeed inspired us. Enjoy your learning process as you notice and continue to internalize the language, meaning, and application of the cognitive assets. Next, we introduce the subject of weaving the cognitive assets into the curriculum of school.

185

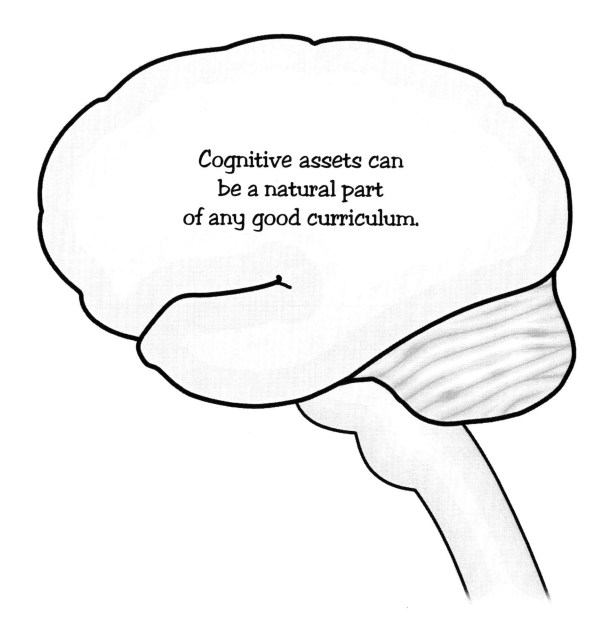

Cognitive assets can
be a natural part
of any good curriculum.

Chapter 9

Cultivating
Cognitive Assets:
Curriculum Connections

Teach a cognitive asset often in your curriculum. Introduce each and teach it consistently for 3 to 5 days. Then use it periodically with the other assets throughout the year.

Introduction

Effective teachers weave a wonderful tapestry of connections of important concepts and curriculum content. Student learning and thinking can grow dramatically when teachers take this process one step further. That is, they consciously and overtly use the language of thinking in connection with specific curriculum areas. For example, teaching students the cognitive asset of systematic search and then connecting it to a framework for developing a book report gives students double benefit. First, they learn how to write better book reports. Second, they are more likely to bridge the cognitive asset of systematic search to other curriculum areas.

In previous chapters, we described the methodology of coaching for thinking, and named and introduced 25 cognitive assets necessary for success in academics and in life. In this chapter, we articulate a framework for coaching the cognitive assets within academic curriculum.

We strongly believe that the use of the 25 cognitive assets named, defined, and described in chapters 6 through 8 make a difference in student success in all academic content areas and in life outside of school. In light of this belief, in this chapter we articulate three aspects of the *Thinking for Results* approach that relate to the making of curriculum connections. First, we speak of the mini-lesson and the cognitive assets. Second, we include the concept of bridging, or connecting to important contexts: academics, life, work, and sometimes the social. Third, we give the framework for developing lessons that integrate these important cognitive assets into daily curriculum. Fourth, we give you a number of lessons that we have used in classrooms across the United States to help students learn to use the important cognitive assets as well as to learn curriculum.

Mini-Lessons

Mini-lessons utilize the explicit language and concepts of the cognitive assets. After we teach the introductory lesson on each cognitive asset, teachers often use what we call mini-lessons to weave the assets into their daily curriculum. The lessons are often 3 to 10 minutes (or less) in length and are integrated into the daily content. When we use this approach after the introduction of each cognitive asset, it is taught within the curriculum (as a cognitive focus) for 3 to 5 days regularly and often throughout the year. For a possible schedule of the introduction and focus period for each asset, see Cognitive Assets Launch Schedule in the appendix. After the 3 to 5 day focus period, the asset is used when appropriate within the school day.

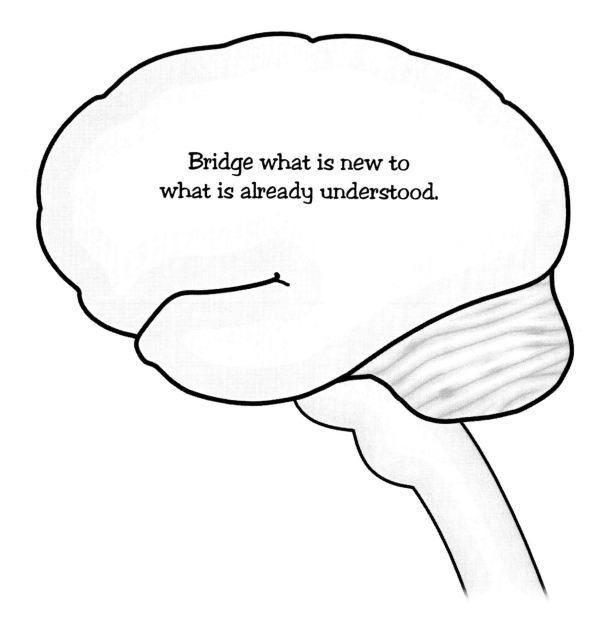

Bridge what is new to
what is already understood.

Bridging

All teachers realize that transfer is one of the primary learning keys! If students learn what is meaningful and important in their lives, we believe it is critical that we guide them to transfer it. To this end we use "bridging" to help make powerful transfer happen. Here's how bridging works in *Thinking for Results*. After each cognitive asset is introduced, there is a bridging component of the lesson. In this part of the lesson, students are encouraged to speak of how the cognitive asset is used in three areas: (a) varied content areas at school, (b) other areas of life including social, and (c) work of their parents and, if they are older students, their work. By making a habit of bridging into these three different areas, the students conceptualize that these cognitive assets are key to their success in all areas of life as well as in all subjects at school.

Lesson Frameworks

In *Thinking for Results* there are two types of lessons. There are introductory lessons where the cognitive assets are introduced to the students. In these lessons, the asset itself is the focus of the lesson. For example, in an introductory lesson on systematic search, we might ask the students to do a web-brainstorming the various ways we can gather information on any given topic. These lessons are usually 15 minutes or longer.

In the other type of lesson, termed a mini-lesson, students use the cognitive asset as they participate in lessons using the curriculum of the classroom. For example, we reinforce the use of systematic search in Language Arts as we explore the various styles of different authors; in mathematics as we examine problems carefully to see which operation we are to perform; in science as we gather information in the directions for an experiment so there will be no mistakes; and in social studies and history as we search for clues about the beginnings of war through the ages. In content across the curriculum and across the grades, we use the language of systematic search so that it is seen as an important aspect of teaching and learning at school.

In both introductory lessons and mini-lessons within the curriculum, students are encouraged to bridge, or connect, to other ways to use each cognitive asset. The usual areas for bridging are varied content areas at school, other areas of life including social, and work of their parents and, if they are older students, their work.

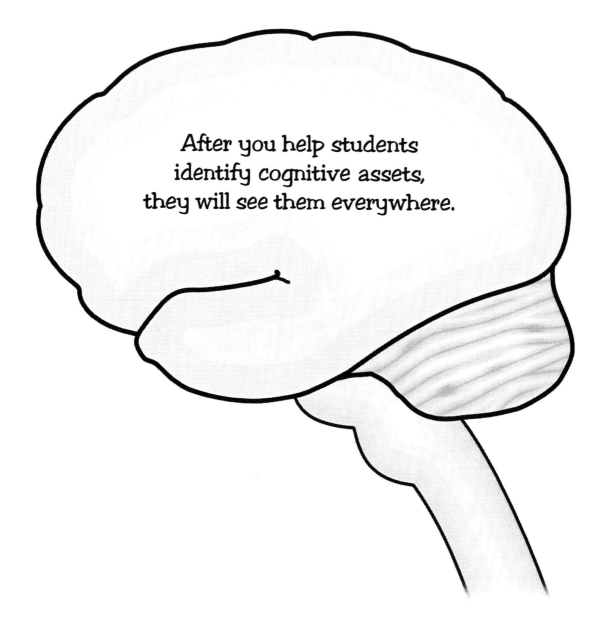

After you help students
identify cognitive assets,
they will see them everywhere.

Using Lessons In Regular and Special Education and Alternative Classrooms

The *Thinking for Results* lessons to teach cognitive assets are best used with *all* students. In our experiences providing workshops and visiting classrooms across the United States, we have found that, at all grade levels of school, many students do not know how to identify and use the cognitive assets as they need to use them to be successful. At the same time, it has been our experience that at-risk student have the most to gain when they begin to master the cognitive assets they need for success. The lesson frameworks may be used with individual children/youth, small groups, or entire classrooms of students. It has been our experience that the assets are usually not taught in traditional education, and the assets are always required in order for students to be able to do well at school.

Examples of Lessons Using Framework

In the following section, we include some mini-lessons that we have collected and used with students of different ages. They are here for the purpose of giving examples of the framework for a lesson that coaches the cognitive assets for learning across various content areas.

Of course, it is up to readers to create their own exciting lessons that use the coaching framework to teach the cognitive assets. Notice the similarities and differences of the mini-lessons. For example, although the cognitive assets and curriculum content vary in each example, clear intent, making meaning, transfer, bridging, and reflection are included in all examples. We encourage you to enjoy creating your own lessons using this format. After using these methods for many years now, we have found that we use this technique without benefit of a formal plan. The purpose of practice using this format is for the technique to become habitual.

193

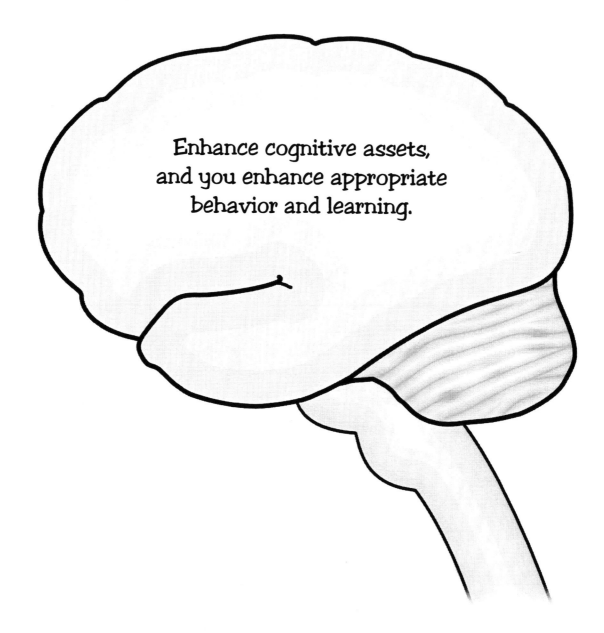

Enhance cognitive assets,
and you enhance appropriate
behavior and learning.

Examples of Nine Lessons

Mini-Lesson
Input Phase – Clear Intent
Changing Student Behavior – Any Level

Note: The content is the students' content. For example, an older student might want to use clear intent to get a car, whereas the student in our example uses clear intent to purchase a bicycle.

This lesson was completed with an individual student who was in a special education class for students with "emotional and behavioral problems." The lesson can also be modified for an entire class and for any age group.

You might be familiar with the Oprah Winfrey Show on television. She speaks often about the importance of intentionality at the center of our lives.

Clear Intent: To help "Mike" use clear intent and understand that he can exercise internal control in his life.

Making Meaning: *"Is there something that you'd like to work toward, Mike?"*

                         "What do you mean?"

                         "I want us to work together so that you have a clear intention to work toward."

                         "Great. I'd like to buy a bicycle."

                         "So, you'd like to buy a bicycle. Do you have the money for a new bike?"

                         "No."

                         "So, does a part of the clear intent need to be saving money?"

                         "Yes. I make $.75 every week from my mom and I sometimes sell lemonade for $.05 a cup."

                         "Ok, so do you have to save your earned money from your mom and your money from selling lemonade to buy a bicycle?"

                         Yes, I know where I can get a used one for $3.50 down the street."

                         "Let's figure how long it will take to save the money to have what you intend."

195

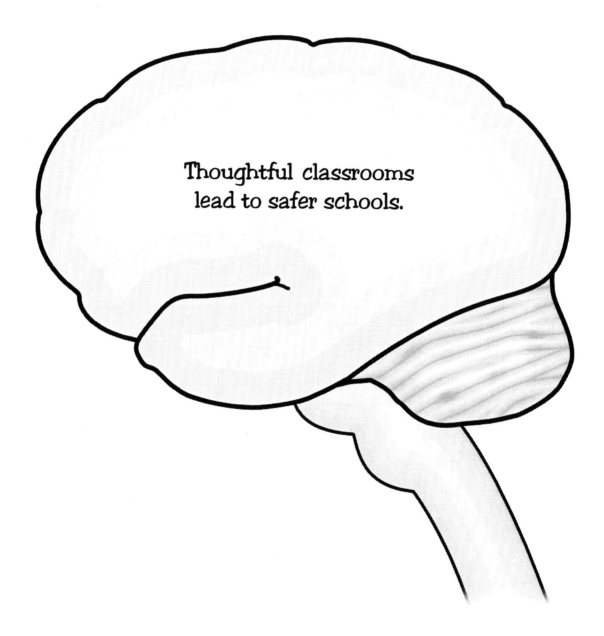

Thoughtful classrooms
lead to safer schools.

Transfer: If we can use clear intent to reach our goals, then we have more control over what happens to us in our lives. We asked the question, "How can we use clear intent at school?" (life, social, and work).

Bridges: School – We can use clear intent to get out of a special education class.

Life –   We can use clear intent to keep our room free from clutter for an amount of time.

Social –   We can use clear intent to make a new friend during the school term.

Work –   We can use clear intent to train for a job that we want in the future.

Reflection: As mentioned, this plan was done with an individual student in a special class. He did in fact use clear intent to achieve his wish of buying a used bicycle. He then used clear intent to develop a plan to join a regular education class with our help. It was a 6 month plan that included his commitment not to fight. He achieved his goal as he intended and was taken out of special education after 6 months. "Mike" was a third-grader at the time he began to use clear intent.

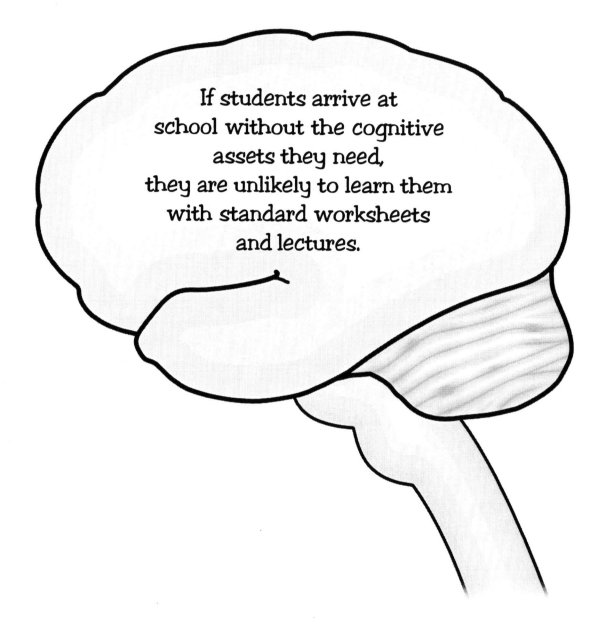

If students arrive at
school without the cognitive
assets they need,
they are unlikely to learn them
with standard worksheets
and lectures.

Mini-Lesson – Input Phase
Making Meaning/Understanding Space
Women's Studies – Adult Women at a University

"The Earth Mother"

Read for Reflection: "We are thankful to our Mother, the Earth, for she gives us all that we need for life. She supports our feet as we walk about upon her. It gives us joy that she continues to care for us as she has from the beginning of time. To our Mother, the Earth, we send greetings and thanks."

Clear Intent:	To help students make meaning through reflection.
Making Meaning:	Do you remember what we have said about the importance of reflection in learning? Good, you remember that reflection helps us understand what we study and helps make meaning. What did we say yesterday about making meaning? Yes, we said that we can find meaning in most every learning activity if we take the time to look and reflect. What meaning have you thought about for our short reading about earth? What meaning does this have for you? Why do we sometimes call our earth "Mother Earth"? How are people related to the earth? How are people who live far apart connected by the earth? How does study of the earth and its far-away peoples give us meaning?
Transfer:	If we develop meaning when we learn, we create more enjoyment for learning.
Bridges:	School – We study people of other cultures and learn about them. Life – We study people of other cultures and learn about them. Social – We enjoy reading about people from other lands, or visiting people in other places when we can.
Reflection:	This lesson seemed enjoyable for many of our university students as they further learned how to reflect to make meaning. The sharing was rich as students spoke of the meaning that "Mother Earth" has for them and how this connection can nurture young and old alike, no matter what life's circumstances bring.

199

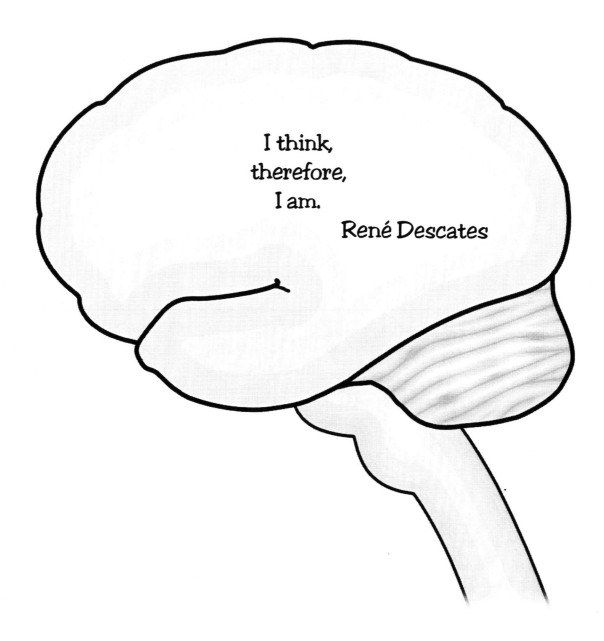

I think,
therefore,
I am.

René Descates

Mini-Lesson – Processing Phase
Problem Definition
Geography/Social Studies – Upper Elementary Grades

In this social studies lesson students explore 19th century life along with the Lewis and Clark expedition as they move west into uncharted territory. They use problem definition to define and understand how the expedition was able to make their way west with the help of Sacajawea, a Native American woman.

From the story of Sacajawea
"A Woman Led the Way"

Clear Intent: To help children learn to explore situations and to identify the problem that needs to be solved.

Making Meaning: Do you remember what we said about problem definition when we introduced it two days ago? Yes, we talked about the importance of this cognitive asset. We also said that sometimes it is hard to see what the problem is at first, it requires reflection. Today we're going to look at a story from history and discover the problem that had to be solved.

Transfer: If we learn to identify problems, then we will be better able to solve them.

Bridges: School – We use problem definition to determine what we need to study for to pass our test in mathematics.
Life – Problem definition helps our family decide when to call someone to help fix our home, for example, when do we need a professional plumber?
Social – We use problem definition to notice what is wrong when our feelings are hurt by a friend.

Reflection: Our first lessons on problem definition were about the identification of our problems. This was the first problem in literature to be analyzed by the students using this cognitive asset. There was some discussion that we use this asset in all aspects of life and at school as we do the other cognitive assets. Another powerful part of this particular lesson was that Sacajawea had to redefine the problem in order to solve it and move forward.

201

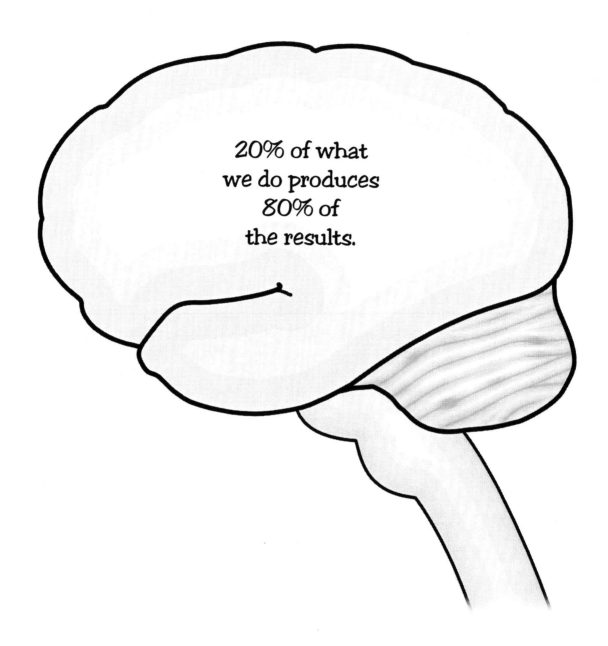

20% of what
we do produces
80% of
the results.

Mini-Lesson – Processing Phase
Summarizing
Reading/Language Arts – Middle School Grades

This Language Arts lesson has summarizing as its focus. Students are asked to create a mind map of the story "Free and Equal" and then summarize the story of a northern and lone slave woman who was the little-mentioned first person to challenge the legality of slavery. After the story is read aloud, the students share the contents of their mind maps with the whole group.

Clear Intent:	To help students use the cognitive asset of summarizing as they learn.
Making Meaning:	Do you remember what it means to summarize when we learn? Yes, we discussed that it is important when we learn to automatically ask ourselves, "What is this about?" We look for the "thread" that pulls a story together when we read. Today, we'll have practice with finding the "thread" or common elements of a story that is important in American history. That is, it is important to all of us.
Transfer:	If we automatically consider "How can I summarize this?" we are able to better understand the importance of what we are learning.
Bridges:	School – We need to know how to summarize when we read a story and study history. Life – We summarize when we go to the movies so that we can share what we saw with others. Social – We use this asset to help us communicate so we don't ramble on.
Reflection:	The teacher makes a group mind map on the board for all to see. Students are then asked to draw a symbol representing Elizabeth ("Mumbet") Freeman from the story.

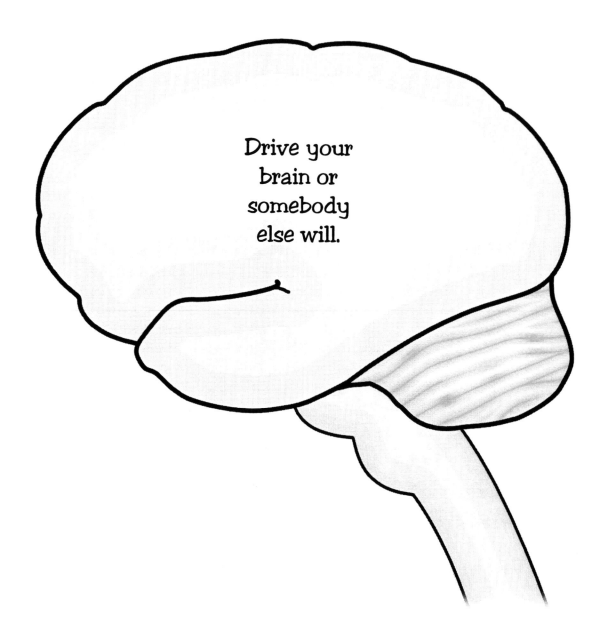

Drive your
brain or
somebody
else will.

Mini-Lesson — Output (Communication) Phase
Thoughtful Behavior
Science – Any Level

Clear Intent: To help students use thoughtful behavior to understand how the brain learns.

Making Meaning: Do you remember our conversation earlier this week when we discussed the importance of thoughtful behavior in our learning? Yes, it is an important aspect of our communication. It helps us to communicate well when we are learning. Today, we will use it to help us learn about the area of the brain that helps us to be thoughtful when we are learning. We will use thoughtful behavior as we learn about this very important part of our brains.

Transfer: If we use thoughtful behavior, then we will be more successful at learning.

Bridges: School – Thoughtful behavior helps us make a good grade on our spelling test.
Life – We use thoughtful behavior to help us do what our parents expect from us.
Social – We use thoughtful behavior to help us communicate better with our friends.
Work – Our parents use thoughtful behavior to express ideas on the job.

Reflection: This science lesson weaves the *Thinking for Results* process with understandings about the brain and learning. As always, the students enjoy learning more about the brain and thinking.

205

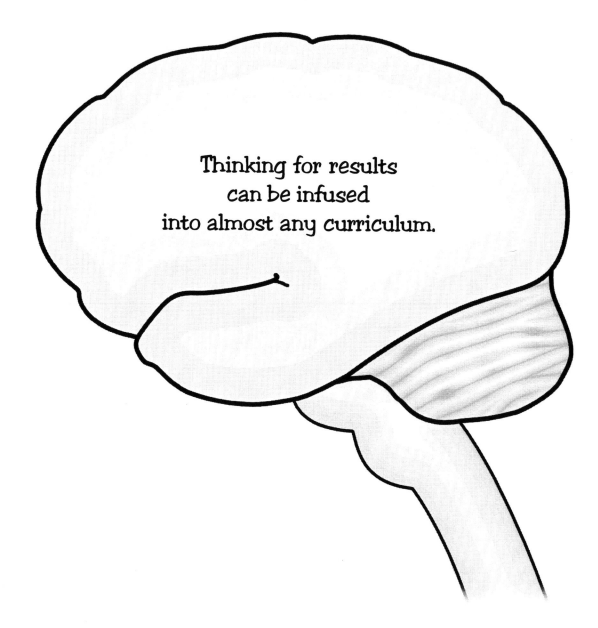

Thinking for results
can be infused
into almost any curriculum.

Principles for Thinking Curricula

One of the most effective ways to keep the joy of teaching alive is to constantly seek ways to bridge *Thinking for Results* to content. Here we would like to share a simple framework that we use to develop curricula.

1. Ask yourself, is it worth teaching? In order to assess the usefulness of the curriculum piece, consider the acronym FDR.

    -   F — Frequency. How often will my students use, or apply, this information?

    -   D — Duration. How long will they use it for when they do use it?

    -   R — Results. What results will the use or application produce?

    For example, let us take the cognitive asset of systematic search at the input phase. Next let us take the Halt - Engage - Anticipate - Replay (H.E.A.R.) strategy for developing good attention skills that lead to an effective systematic search. Finally, let us run it through our rubric, FDR. First, consider frequency. How often will my students use, or apply, this information? In school and in life we listen almost every waking hour of every day. Second, consider duration. How long will they use it for when they do use it? We listen for longer periods of time than we do almost any other activity, especially at school. Third, consider results. What results will the use or application produce? Research suggests that the ability to truly listen well is key to success in school and in life. Studies also indicate that most people only listen at a 25% efficiency level.

    To summarize, in this example is the cognitive asset of systematic search through listening worth teaching? We undoubtedly see that it is. This is the process that the authors used to select the cognitive assets to be included in this program.

2. How does this curriculum connect to the lives of the students? We use the following three parameters to examine this principle.

    -   Is it *meaningful* in the minds of my students? Does it make sense to them? How can I make it both meaningful and sensible to them?

    -   Is it *relevant* to my students? Does it relate to the everyday lives of my students? How can I help them relate to it?

    -   Is it *important* to my students? How does it impact the lives of my students? How can I help them see it's importance?

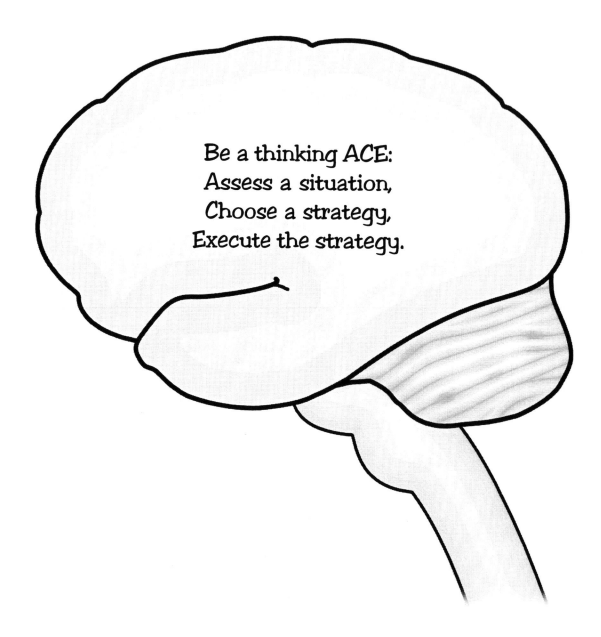

Be a thinking ACE:
Assess a situation,
Choose a strategy,
Execute the strategy.

For example, let us again take the H.E.A.R. strategy for developing good attention skills that lead to an effective systematic search. We now take it through our rubric, M.R.I.: Meaningful, Relevant, and Important. Most students know by school age that it is extremely important to be able to listen at school, so this strategy has meaning for them because it is necessary every day! They also know that passing school and being able to behave appropriately is something that each and every one of them needs to be able to do. Thus, they know that listening is relevant. Finally, they know that it is important to master this very needed skill in order to do well at school, and in life.

To summarize, the H.E.A.R. strategy that develops our students' skill at listening passes the M.R.I. rubric for assessing curriculum. This rubric, M.R.I., assesses curricula for "connect-ability" to the lives of students. In the next chapter, we explore HealthMath as another curriculum example for thinking classrooms.

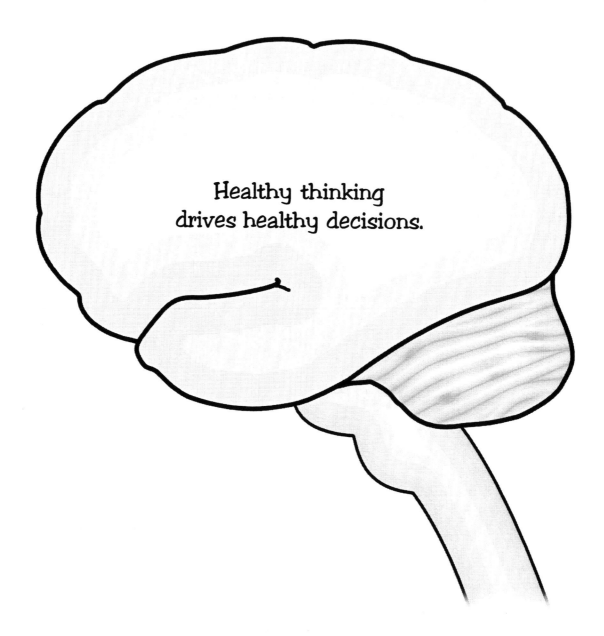

Healthy thinking
drives healthy decisions.

Chapter 10

Thinking for Health

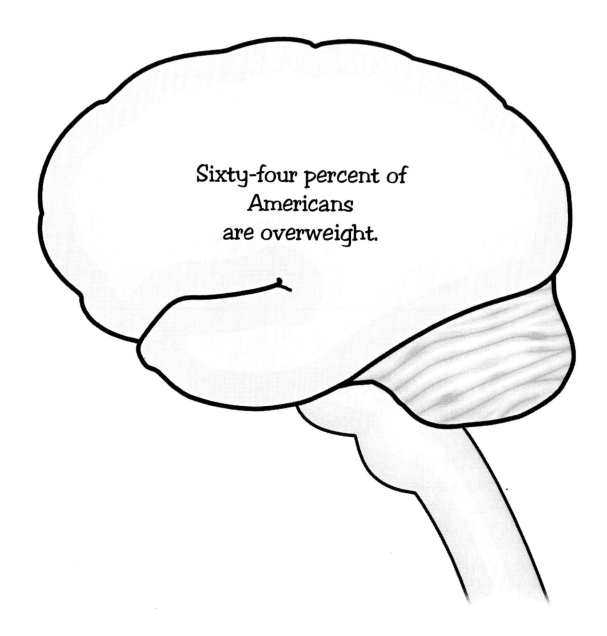

Sixty-four percent of
Americans
are overweight.

Introduction: Weaving the Assets With Curriculum

Many historians would say that in the little red schoolhouse of old, the focus of school seems to have been primarily on content: reading, writing, and arithmetic. That was, however, during the Industrial Age. In the 1970s and 1980s, the thinking movement came into bloom with the full arrival of the Information Age. Then, more and more homes and offices became equipped with computers, and the information highway was accessible to many. This situation created a need, noticed by many educators and parents, for students to have the thinking prerequisites necessary to organize the massive amount of information they receive daily from texts, newspapers, and even games!

Then, the battle began. As often happens in education, warring camps cried, "We must teach only content!" and from the other side, "We must teach thinking instead!" However, we believe that today it is critically important that schools must teach both well. That is, teach important cognitive assets and interesting and necessary curricula that is worthy of thinking time.

In this section, we present an example of curriculum, HealthMath, and some of the cognitive assets that we often teach with this content. With the topic of HealthMath, we have found that, depending upon our intent in the lesson, it is possible to teach most, if not all 25 of the cognitive assets shared in Chapter 5. However, here we consider four of the assets: Clear Intent, Systematic Search, Using Two or More Sources of Information, and Working Memory. Notice how we are offering ideas for the weaving of important curriculum with the necessary cognitive assets. This is, of course, only one example of the many ways the cognitive assets may be taught. Although we often teach HealthMath as an entire unit of study, there are examples of lessons and mini-lessons to teach the cognitive assets elsewhere.

About HealthMath

Your health and the health of those you love is a precious gift that needs to be protected. By taking appropriate actions, you can reduce the risk of illness and perhaps even slow the rate of aging. Research suggests that how you think, eat, and exercise account for up to 70% of the rate at which you age. At the same time, there is an explosion of research on nutrition, exercise, stress, attitude, and emotional intelligence that may influence health and vitality. Meanwhile, billions of dollars are spent advertising junk food and less than healthy lifestyles.

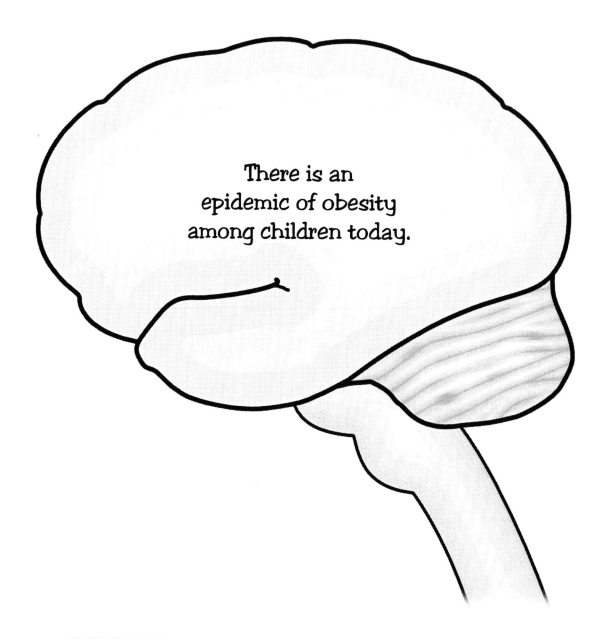

There is an
epidemic of obesity
among children today.

A Context for Thinking

Perhaps one of the most important health decisions you can make is to commit to being personally responsible for inputting, processing, and outputting health knowledge. For example, the authors spend hundreds of hours each year reading, researching, and reflecting on new knowledge on wellness and health. We then translate this into a systematic plan and devote the cognitive asset of finishing power to following through on a daily basis. It is a lot of work, but is incredibly rewarding!

Just as no one can help us build muscle by doing weight training for us, no one can help us build the cognitive assets we need by doing the research and thinking for us. This chapter is a brief introduction to Thinking for Health, with the focus being the <u>process</u> of building cognitive assets using health knowledge as sample content. If you wish to learn more about health content for use in your own life or in the classroom, you are encouraged to cultivate the asset of systematic search and make use of fabulous Web sites such as web.md, jama.org, and to look for heath links from brainsmart.com. As you do this you will be modeling powerful learning and the use of cognitive assets for your family and your students.

Your health and the health of those you love is a precious gift that needs to be protected. By taking appropriate actions you can reduce the risk of illness and perhaps even slow the rate of aging. Research suggests that how you think, eat, and exercise account for up to 70% of the rate at which you age. At the same time there is an explosion of research on nutrition, exercise, stress, attitude and emotional intelligence, all of which may influence health and vitality. Children today see thousands of television commercials each year. Many of these are aimed specifically at influencing young people to consume food and drink that is high in sugar, trans fat, and calories, while low in nutritional value. As desire for these products increases, so does the ease of putting the process of such products within easy reach for children. Vending machines are now commonplace in schools, and many menus reflect the fast-food habits of society outside school. A growing body of medical research suggests that our daily decisions about how we think, eat, and exercise have a profound impact on our health and even the rate at which we age. To this end, cultivating cognitive assets that support and sustain a healthy life style could be seen as a key priority for the education of students in our schools. It might be said that if our children are born unarmed, then cultivating minds that think well is a key system of defense against the marketing assault they need to withstand if they are to make healthy decisions.

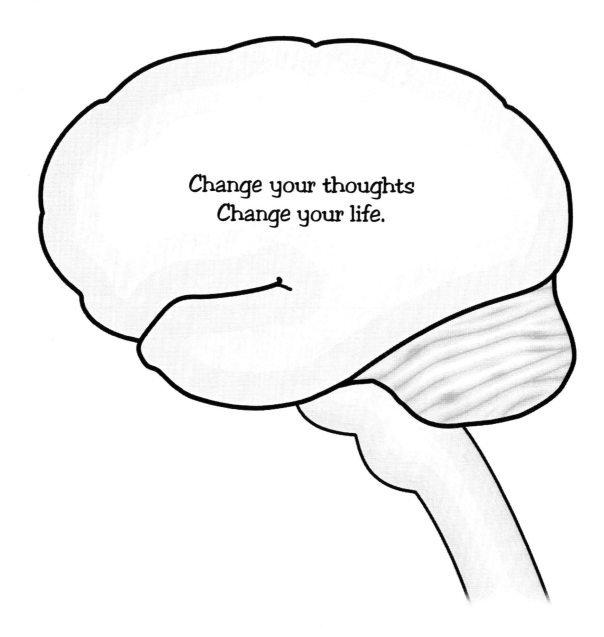

Change your thoughts
Change your life.

Consider the following information:

1. Childhood obesity has almost tripled since the 1960s.
2. Seventy five percent of obese children become obese adults.
3. Obesity increases the risks of illness.
4. Obesity is linked to increased risk of depression.
5. Type 2 diabetes is growing at an alarming rate among children.
6. In a Gallop poll, parents put health as priority one for their children's schools.
7. Exercise and recess are being cut back in our schools.
8. Soda and candy are sold in vending machines in schools.
9. Many schools now have fast food available
10. Children see as many as 40,000 commercials per year. Many are for less than nutritious food.

Against the background of these 10 statements, it is clear that societal forces are putting our children at risk of serious illness by encouraging a sedentary lifestyle and poor nutrition. Taking what we have learned so far, let us explore which assets might have an impact in this critical area.

One can of soda
has 10 spoons of sugar.

A Curriculum Example: Thinking for Health with HealthMath™

The HealthMATH™ Mission

Research from the classrooms with the highest mathematics test scores in the world indicate that students must have extensive practice with real-world applications of mathematical principles to excel on standardized tests. Our mission is to equip every student with the ability to think critically and mathematically about what they eat and how they exercise so that they build a healthy brain-body system and a lifelong mastery of mathematics. This is critical today as obesity has doubled since 1991.

The BrainSMART HealthMATH™ Process

We support teachers and parents as they help students to develop a strong number sense about the relationship between what they eat, how they exercise and the impact on their energy level and wellness. For example, students could be asked to create a new labeling system for food products that would support healthy decisions by consumers. They would then create advertising campaigns to research the effectiveness of their work. Students would also be encouraged to read labels and pack their own healthy lunches and snacks. Students discover key information and are able to answer questions like:

1. How many calories worth of exercise do you need to burn a pound of body fat?
2. If you consumed 192 calories less per day, how many pounds could you lose in a year?
3. How many spoonfuls of sugar are there in a 12 oz. can of soda?
4. How far would you have to walk to burn the calories from one can of soda?
5. How many calories does a pound of body fat burn per day?
6. How many calories does a pound of muscle burn per day?
7. If you eat the recommended daily fruits and vegetables, how many is that a week?
8. How many calories do you burn by walking a mile?
9. How many calories do you need to burn per week to maximize health?
10. How many pounds of sugar does the average American consume in a year?

Answers: (1) 3,500 (2) 20 pounds (3) 10 (4) 1.5 (5) 3 (6) 150 (7) 63 (8) 100 (9) 3,500 (10) 156

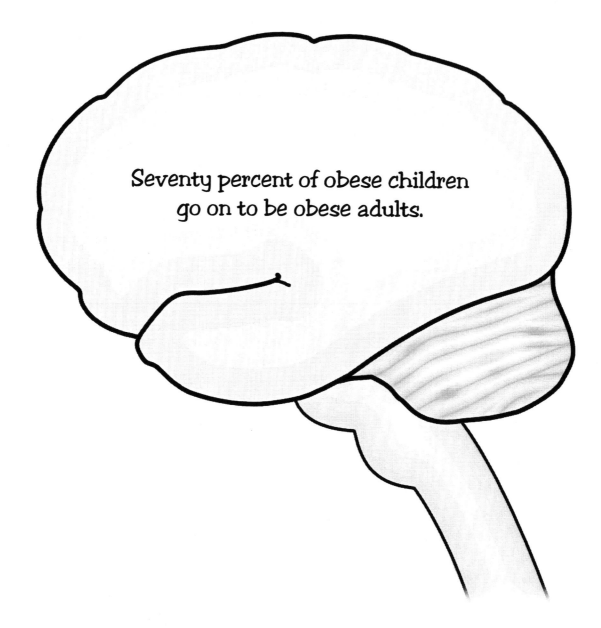

Seventy percent of obese children
go on to be obese adults.

♀ Cognitive Asset – Clear Intent

Clear Intent - Applied in Context
Academic Content - Mathematics and Health
Example of Cultivating Cognitive Assets in Curriculum

Definition: Clear intent is sustaining a clear sense of one's intentions are in each situation. For example, teachers who have the clear intention of increasing student learning by constantly improving their instructional skills will tend to increase their effectiveness and achieve their goals.

Asset Question: "What clear intent do I want my students to have when they face their daily exercise and eating decisions?"

If students have the facts about the impact of their eating and exercising decisions and their clear intent is to stay strong, smart, and energized, they have a better chance of staying healthy. Clear intent focuses the brain on the goal, and decisions and actions create movement towards the goal. In the absence of positive clear intent, the natural temptation is to just do what feels good and requires the least effort.

One of the best predictors of life success is what is known as the Marshmallow Test, which has been developed at Harvard. Here children are asked to resist the temptation to eat a marshmallow for a period of time. Those children that have the capacity to have clear intent and the ability to delay gratification tend to do better in life than those who do not have clear intent and give in to their impulses. Most of what is truly important in life requires having a clear intent for achieving a goal, and having the willpower to delay gratification in the short term in return for a greater gain as the intention is realized.

Activity

Ask students to write a statement of clear intent. Ask them to write a goal for health or fitness. For example, students might write, "I will run a mile in 5 minutes." Or, "I will walk three miles a day," or, "I will do weight training three times a week."

221

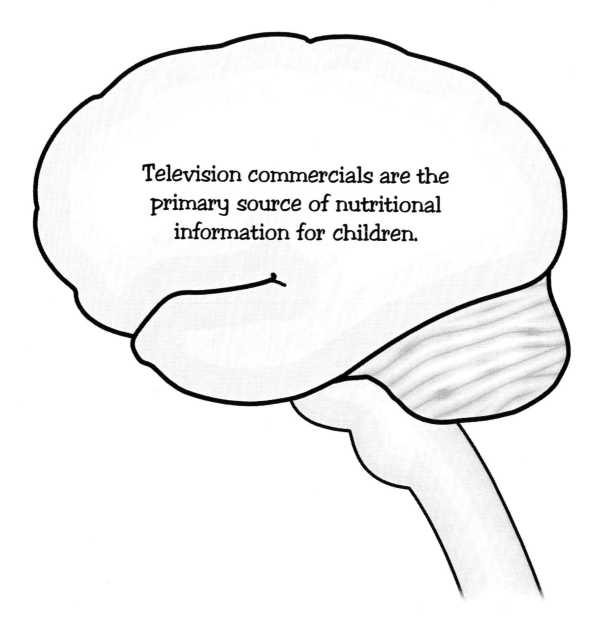

Television commercials are the primary source of nutritional information for children.

💡 Cognitive Asset - Systematic Search

Systematic Search Applied in Context
Academic Content – Mathematics and Health

Definition: Systematic search is appropriate exploratory behavior that is organized in a way that leads to a planned and well-expressed response.

Asset Question: "How can I be systematic about finding information on using exercise and nutrition for supporting health?"

Ask your students to systematically seek out well-researched information on nutrition and health. In the United States today, 61% of the population is overweight and 27% are obese. Understand that there is a trillion dollar food industry that is actively promoting high consumption of foods. The body can consume 2,200-2,900 calories per day without gaining weight. In the United States, 3,500 calories worth of food are produced every day. The food industry must aggressively promote their products to sell this amount. To this end, they spend heavily on advertising to inform the public of the benefits of their products.

Against this backdrop, the average person is a passive consumer of information that is offered and will likely end up with information that gets them into the 61% club (overweight).

Fortunately, there is an explosion of cutting-edge research on nutrition and its impact on health and wellness. If they can cultivate the asset of systematic search, students (and we teachers) can find this information, validate it, and put it into practice.

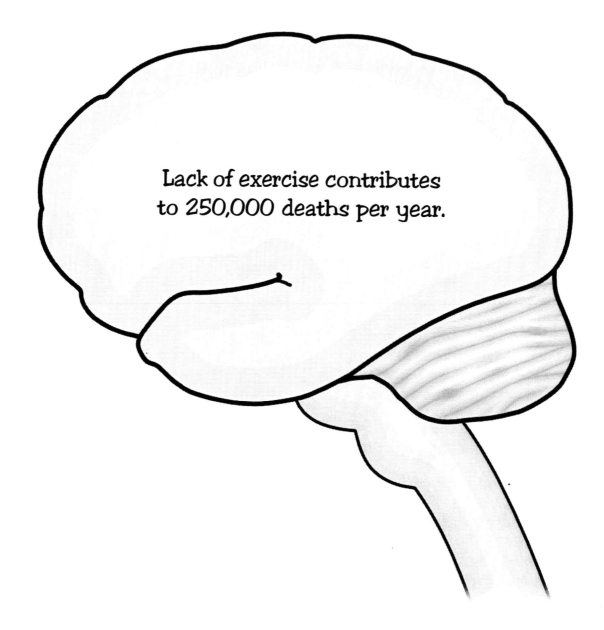

Lack of exercise contributes
to 250,000 deaths per year.

Activities

1. Set a systematic search target such as follows, "I want to know the impact of high carbohydrate diets on weight and health."

2. Explore Web sites such as RealAge.com and WebMD.com.

3. Hone skills in finding Web sites. For example, systematically search and find the Center for Science in the Public Interest.

4. When you go out to eat, notice what menu items do not contain processed carbohydrates, such as white bread, cookies, rolls, white rice, white pasta, and chips, which have all been processed.

5. Reflect on the results of your search. Set up a new target.

We consume around
four pounds of food per day,
about 40% in the form of
dairy products.

♀ Cognitive Asset - Using Two or More Sources of Information

Using Two or More Sources of Information - Applied in Context
Academic Content – Mathematics and Health

Definition: This asset is the skill of using more than one source of information to successfully solve problems.

Asset Question: "How can I get information about nutrition from at least two sources of information?"

As the saying goes, "Never ask your barber if he thinks you need a haircut." In this context it is clear that your barber will tell you that you need a haircut. It would make sense to check the mirror as another source. Another source might be to check with a trusted friend. When it comes to thinking for health, the same is true. For example, many of us have seen the milk moustache commercials. Brittany Spears is now pitching milk to a new generation. The milk marketers are the source of information for these commercials.

The Harvard School of Public Health and Harvard Medical School are other sources. Dr. Walter Willet from Harvard suggests that we do not need to consume dairy foods for calcium. We can, in fact, eat calcium-fortified foods and get the boost of calcium that we need. Consider this. We consume around four pounds of food per day. Around 40% of that is in the form of dairy foods. A good question is, "Why do we think we need to consume dairy foods?" The answer that is wired into your brain is, "For the calcium." Another question is, "Why do we need to eat such large quantities of dairy foods to get the calcium?" The answer that is wired into our brains is, "To prevent osteoporosis." However, sources outside the dairy industry suggest that the countries with the highest calcium consumption suffer the highest rates of osteoporosis and other bone-related illnesses. A glass of milk is 49% fat. Twelve ounces of milk has as much saturated fat as eight strips of bacon. This is just one example of needing the asset of using two or more sources of information.

Twelve oz. of milk has as
much fat as
eight strips of bacon.

Activities

1. Ask students to list the foods they eat in a day.

2. Ask them to identify which are dairy foods.

3. Ask to name the benefits of dairy foods.

4. Ask students to name their information sources.

5. Ask them to identify the motivation that could be behind those sources of information.

6. Ask them to name other sources that could be useful.

7. Ask students to do an Internet search about dairy foods and health.

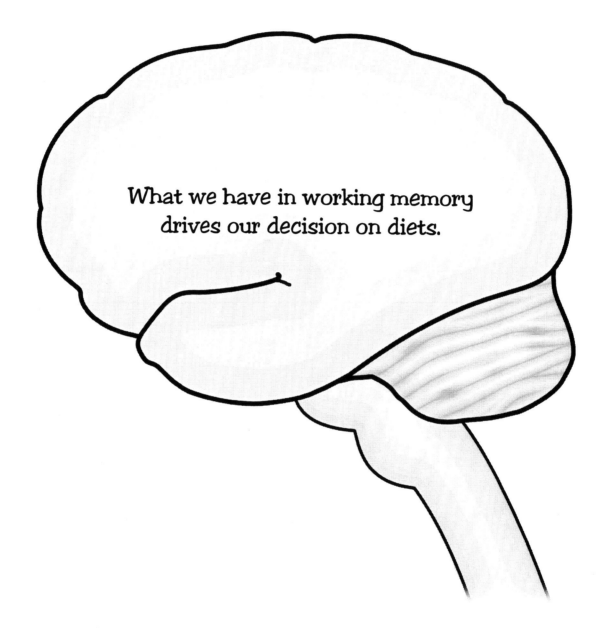

What we have in working memory
drives our decision on diets.

💡 Cognitive Asset - Working Memory

Working Memory - Applied in Context
Academic Content – Mathematics and Health

Definition: Working memory is the skill of consciously choosing what to retain in long term memory and selecting appropriate tools to retain and recall information to achieve desired results.

Asset Question: "What tools can I use to remember key information about nutrition at critical times such as when I eat and shop for food?"

Have you ever noticed that you seem to be able to remember key information about nutrition and food right up until it is time to decide what to eat? Suddenly your cognitive system shuts down and your emotional system says *yummy*. Your brain has deleted all that good information. If we eat three meals and two snacks per day, those five decisions strongly influence our health destiny.

Advertisers work hard to get their products in your working memory when you reach those decision points. For example, research suggests that a high carbohydrate meal wears off after a while and leaves us feeling hungry. Advertisers take advantage of this and often run commercials at around 9 p.m., when we start to get hungry after our evening meal, to wire their brands into our memory systems.

Consider this scenario at your house in the evening. You are feeling hungry. You see an ad for pizza. The next night you feel hungry and see an ad for pizza. The same thing happens over and over, night after night. Then one day you are driving along and see a pizza sign and feel hungry. The ad people have wired it in!

How do we then rewire our thinking and memory? This is how! Use the same system and create your own jingle and commercial in your brain. Consider the following as one example: *White Carbs Add Weight – Keep Those White Carbs Off My Plate.*

231

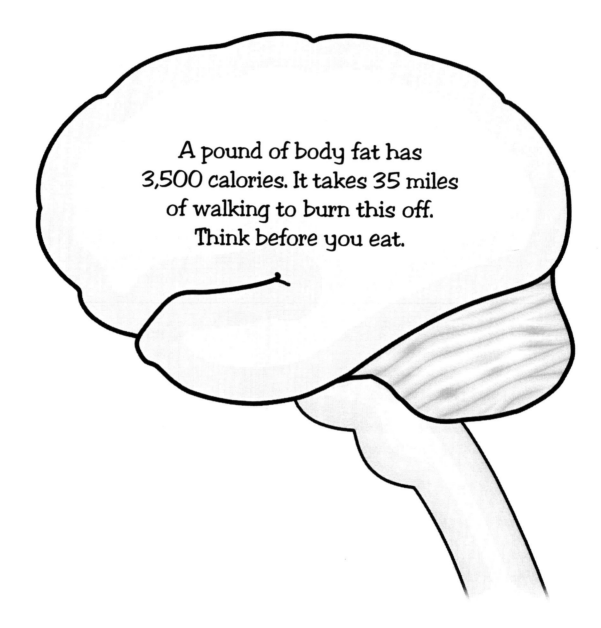

A pound of body fat has
3,500 calories. It takes 35 miles
of walking to burn this off.
Think before you eat.

Activities

Create slogans and commercials to run in your brain when you are hungry, or use these ideas. Remember - practice makes permanent. Wire the right information into your working memory.

1. To remember to reduce white processed carbs consumption: *White Carbs Add Weight – Keep Those White Carbs Off My Plate*

2. To remember to eat lean protein and vegetables for high energy and fat burning: *I'm a lean, fat-burning machine. I'm eating my protein and beautiful greens.*

3. To remember to drink water instead of soda: *One can of soda has 10 spoons of sugar. To burn that sugar I would walk for half an hour.*

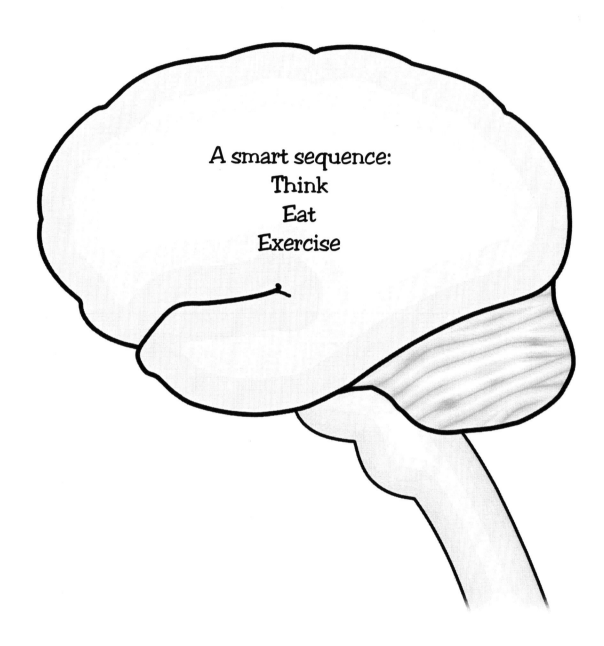

A smart sequence:
Think
Eat
Exercise

Other Important Cognitive Assets and Creating HealthMath Curriculum

As you use HealthMath as part of your curriculum, or as you further develop your own curricula for thinking, consider ways in which the HealthMath Curriculum and teaching of cognitive assets are woven together. The important overarching concept to remember is that in the case of HealthMath and the cognitive assets, both are important in the learners' lives. That is to say that both the content of HealthMath and the learning of the cognitive assets are critically important to the students' well-being. Would you agree? Another important overarching concept is that the assets may be taught with any content area that you teach!

Below are other cognitive assets and guiding questions for their use within the HealthMath curriculum. Remember that we are offering these as but one example of the use of the cognitive assets within curriculum. Feel free to use the HealthMath example in your teaching. However, our clear intent is to offer HealthMath as an example to inspire you to further create your own exciting curriculum for thinking!

Other Cognitive Assets Used in Curriculum

- **Practical Optimism**

  How important is practical optimism in believing that making good decisions about eating and exercising will lead to feeling healthy and energized?

- **Making Meaning**

  What is the role of meaning when it comes to reading and understanding labels? For example, a can of soda has 40 grams of sugar; how many spoons of sugar would that be?

- **Systematic Search**

  How does reading a variety of material related to nutrition and health in books and on the Internet help lead to better decisions?

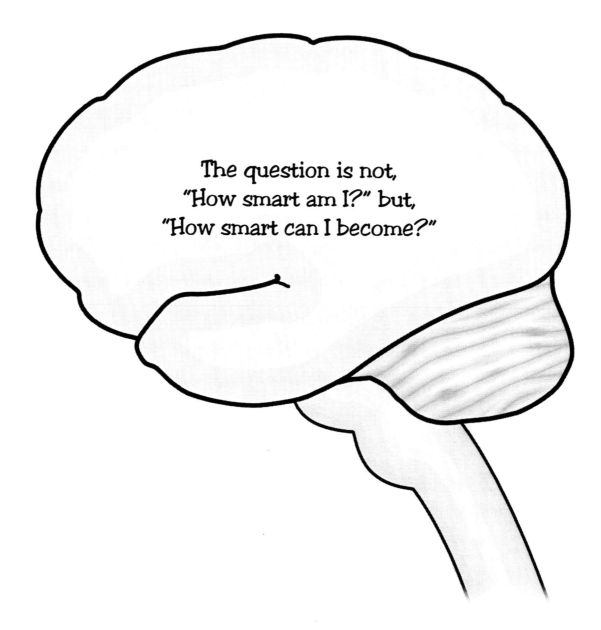

The question is not,
"How smart am I?" but,
"How smart can I become?"

- **Systematic Planning**

  How does knowing the calories in certain foods and the amount of exercise to burn these calories enter into the planning process?

- **Classification**

  How does correct classification of food and drink into categories that provide high nutrition/low calories and low nutrition/high calories impact healthy eating decisions?

- **Effective Expression**

  In what ways does the asset of effective expression lead to negotiating the opportunity for healthy eating and exercising around peers?

- **Understanding Time**

  How does the ability to estimate time for exercise to burn calories influence health?

- **Understanding Space**

  In what ways does knowing how many calories are burned by walking a mile help build a healthy lifestyle?

- **Point of View**

  From what point of view do advertisers of high-sugar and high-trans-fat foods approach designing television commercials?

- **Summarizing**

  How do television commercials summarize (in a very short time) a compelling message?

Appendix A

BrainObics™ "Tuning up your Body Brain System"

SMART*cross*

- Arms cross in a "V" with hands up at shoulder height
- Legs cross at the same time
- Alternate

SKY*cross*

- Hands cross above the head
- Legs cross
- Alternate

KNEE*cross*

- Hands crossed
- Raise and tap knee
- Alternate

EAGLE*cross*

- Hands across chest with thumbs crossed
- Legs crossed
- Breathe deeply
- Focus on what you appreciate

READING*eyes*

- Cross thumbs to make a "V"
- Move thumbs in a sideways eight
- Look through the "V"

I FEEL *good*

- Rub hands together
- Throw hands in the air
- Say "I feel good"
- Have thumb in fist, bring down with a "yes"

Appendix B

Thinking for Results Assessment

Do your students...

1. Reflect, monitor and adjust their thinking when appropriate?
   Metacognition

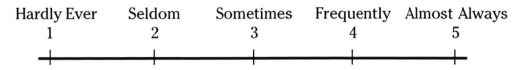

Input

2. Appear clear about what they want to achieve when they begin a task?
   Clear Intent

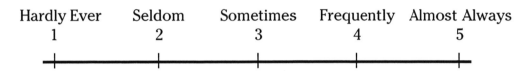

3. Proactively seek out ways to learn more?
   Initiative

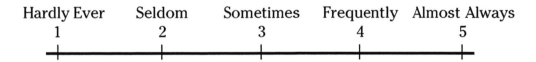

4. Persist with tasks even after failure?
   Practical Optimism

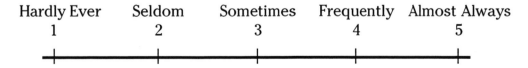

5. Seek out important information in an organized way?
   Systematic Search

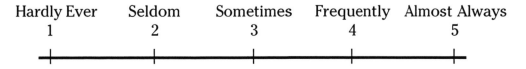

6. Have the skill of paying attention to what they need to in order to succeed at a task?
    Selective Attention

Hardly Ever	Seldom	Sometimes	Frequently	Almost Always
1	2	3	4	5

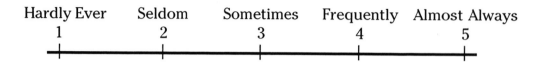

7. Spontaneously look for similarities and differences when problem solving?
    Making Comparisons

Hardly Ever	Seldom	Sometimes	Frequently	Almost Always
1	2	3	4	5

8. Use a variety of sources of information before reaching conclusions?
    Using 2 or More Sources of Information

Hardly Ever	Seldom	Sometimes	Frequently	Almost Always
1	2	3	4	5

9. Plan time carefully when taking tests so that each question can be given appropriate time?
    Understanding Time

Hardly Ever	Seldom	Sometimes	Frequently	Almost Always
1	2	3	4	5

10. Keep their desks clean and tidy?
    Understanding Space

Hardly Ever	Seldom	Sometimes	Frequently	Almost Always
1	2	3	4	5

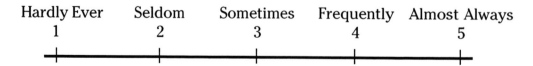

Process

11. Effectively define problems so that an appropriate solution may be sought?
Problem Definition

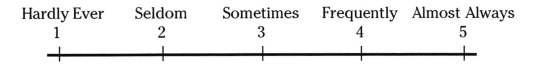

Hardly Ever   Seldom   Sometimes   Frequently   Almost Always
1   2   3   4   5

12. Make connections between different content areas of study and between school and life applications?
Making Connections

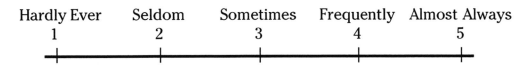

Hardly Ever   Seldom   Sometimes   Frequently   Almost Always
1   2   3   4   5

13. Do well at classifying information into suitable categories?
Classification

Hardly Ever   Seldom   Sometimes   Frequently   Almost Always
1   2   3   4   5

14. Change their approach to solving a problem when their strategies are not working?
Cognitive Flexibility

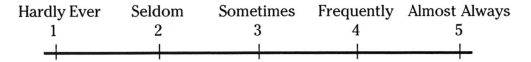

Hardly Ever   Seldom   Sometimes   Frequently   Almost Always
1   2   3   4   5

15. Plan well a sequence of steps needed to solve a problem?
Systematic Planning

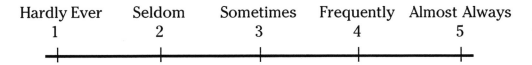

Hardly Ever   Seldom   Sometimes   Frequently   Almost Always
1   2   3   4   5

16. Read others' nonverbal cues well and maintain appropriate behavior?
Using Cues Appropriately

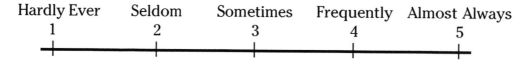

Hardly Ever	Seldom	Sometimes	Frequently	Almost Always
1	2	3	4	5

17. Defend own answers based on logic?
Making Inferences/Hypothetical Thinking

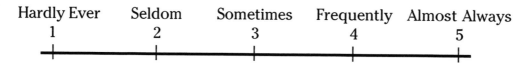

Hardly Ever	Seldom	Sometimes	Frequently	Almost Always
1	2	3	4	5

18. Reliably recall important information?
Working Memory

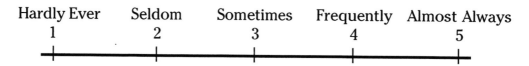

Hardly Ever	Seldom	Sometimes	Frequently	Almost Always
1	2	3	4	5

19. Find importance and relevance in what is being studied?
Making Meaning

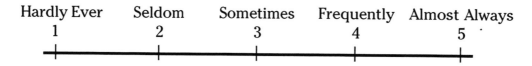

Hardly Ever	Seldom	Sometimes	Frequently	Almost Always
1	2	3	4	5

20. Clearly and succinctly summarize information?
Summarizing

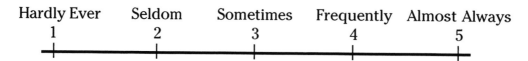

Hardly Ever	Seldom	Sometimes	Frequently	Almost Always
1	2	3	4	5

Output

21. Appear to be empathetic to the points of view of others?
Understanding Point of View

Hardly Ever	Seldom	Sometimes	Frequently	Almost Always
1	2	3	4	5

22. Make minimal corrections and erasures?
Thoughtful Behavior

Hardly Ever	Seldom	Sometimes	Frequently	Almost Always
1	2	3	4	5

23. Contribute positively to classroom discussions?
Effective Expression

Hardly Ever	Seldom	Sometimes	Frequently	Almost Always
1	2	3	4	5

24. Risk public speaking in the classroom?
Appropriate Courage

Hardly Ever	Seldom	Sometimes	Frequently	Almost Always
1	2	3	4	5

25. Have the drive to sustain effort until important tasks are completed?
Finishing Power

Hardly Ever	Seldom	Sometimes	Frequently	Almost Always
1	2	3	4	5

26. Learn from mistakes and success and seldom repeat the same mistakes?
Learning from Experience

Hardly Ever	Seldom	Sometimes	Frequently	Almost Always
1	2	3	4	5

Appendix C

Example Format for
Introduction of Any Cognitive Asset

We ask ourselves these 4 guiding questions:

- How will my students know that I sincerely **care** for them want them to have joyful and successful lives, and believe that learning this cognitive asset is necessary if they are to have a good outcome at school?

- What is my **clear intent** in this lesson? For example, I want my students to understand that systematic search is key to academic and life success and that they can master the process of systematic search.

- How will my students **make meaning** from this lesson? For example, I will be enthusiastic and ask questions to help them connect systematic search to important areas.

- How will I help them **transfer** the learning to other important areas of academics and in their lives? For example, as we learn about this asset, I will ask them where they will use systematic search at school, home, and how their parents or other adults might use it.

Additionally, as we teach for thinking, and we are careful to include exercises such as BrainObics and healthy snacks in our day. When we think using the cognitive assets, it is important to take care to treat our bodies well by eating healthy and exercising throughout the day.

Appendix D

Sample Launch Schedule for Cognitive Assets

Including the S.M.A.R.T. Model

We have found that for educators who have learned strategies in the BrainSMART model, they might begin by focusing on each of the 5 components of the SMART model prior to this schedule. For example, week 1 might be when the teacher introduces and amplifies the importance of positive states in the classroom. Week 2 might be when the teacher introduces and focuses on the meaning aspect of the SMART model, and so on through the five keys. If you choose introduce SMART first, then week 1 below becomes week 6; week 2 becomes week 7, and so on through the entire schedule.

Use of *Thinking for Results* Assessment

It is highly recommended that the cognitive assessment tool is used before educators begin to introduce and coach the assets. Then after they are introduced and used in mini-lessons throughout the year, the assessment should be used again to examine coaching effectiveness. In this manner, the assessment is used as a tool for self-reflection by the teacher/coach.

After 25 Weeks

After each asset is introduced and used throughout the week of the introduction, it may be used as is needed at anytime to reinforce the use as the teacher and students feel it is necessary. At the end of the 25 week period, the cognitive assets may be used together in any pattern that the teacher deems necessary.

With Experience, Do It Your Way

In addition, it should be noted that this plan is but one example of how the assets may be taught. As you teach the assets, feel free to modify the plan based on your learning experiences as you teach by using this approach. And, last but not least, remember to celebrate all successes, some large, and some baby steps.

Schedule for Teaching Cognitive Assets

S	M	T	W	T	F	S
Week 1	Teach an introductory lesson on Clear Intent. Use it in mini-lessons throughout the week to begin to install the use of this asset within your students. Celebrate the new learning power of the class through the use of this asset.					
Week 2	Teach an introductory lesson on Practical Optimism. Use it in mini-lessons throughout the week to begin to install the use of this asset within your students. Celebrate the new learning power of the class through the use of this asset.					
Week 3	Teach an introductory lesson on Initiative. Use it in mini-lessons throughout the week to begin to install the use of this asset within your students. Celebrate the new learning power of the class through the use of this asset.					
Week 4	Teach an introductory lesson on Systematic Search. Use it in mini-lessons throughout the week to begin to install the use of this asset within your students. Celebrate the new learning power of the class through the use of this asset.					
Week 5	Teach an introductory lesson on Using Two or More Sources of Information. Use it in mini-lessons throughout the week to begin to install the use of this asset within your students. Celebrate the new learning power of the class through the use of this asset.					

S	M	T	W	T	F	S
Week 6	Teach an introductory lesson on Understanding Space. Use it in mini-lessons throughout the week to begin to install the use of this asset within your students. Celebrate the new learning power of the class through the use of this asset.					
Week 7	Teach an introductory lesson on Selective Attention. Use it in mini-lessons throughout the week to begin to install the use of this asset within your students. Celebrate the new learning power of the class through the use of this asset.					
Week 8	Teach an introductory lesson on Making Comparisons. Use it in mini-lessons throughout the week to begin to install the use of this asset within your students. Celebrate the new learning power of the class through the use of this asset.					
Week 9	Teach an introductory lesson on Understanding Time. Use it in mini-lessons throughout the week to begin to install the use of this asset within your students. Celebrate the new learning power of the class through the use of this asset.					
Week 10	Teach an introductory lesson on Problem Definition. Use it in mini-lessons throughout the week to begin to install the use of this asset within your students. Celebrate the new learning power of the class through the use of this asset.					

251

S	M	T	W	T	F	S
Week 11	Teach an introductory lesson on Classification. Use it in mini-lessons throughout the week to begin to install the use of this asset within your students. Celebrate the new learning power of the class through the use of this asset.					
Week 12	Teach an introductory lesson on Making Connections. Use it in mini-lessons throughout the week to begin to install the use of this asset within your students. Celebrate the new learning power of the class through the use of this asset.					
Week 13	Teach an introductory lesson on Systematic Planning. Use it in mini-lessons throughout the week to begin to install the use of this asset within your students. Celebrate the new learning power of the class through the use of this asset.					
Week 14	Teach an introductory lesson on Cognitive Flexibility. Use it in mini-lessons throughout the week to begin to install the use of this asset within your students. Celebrate the new learning power of the class through the use of this asset.					
Week 15	Teach an introductory lesson on Using Cues Appropriately. Use it in mini-lessons throughout the week to begin to install the use of this asset within your students. Celebrate the new learning power of the class through the use of this asset.					

S	M	T	W	T	F	S
Week 16	Teach an introductory lesson on Making Inferences/ Hypothetical Thinking. Use it in mini-lessons throughout the week to begin to install the use of this asset within your students. Celebrate the new learning power of the class through the use of this asset.					
Week 17	Teach an introductory lesson on Working Memory. Use it in mini-lessons throughout the week to begin to install the use of this asset within your students. Celebrate the new learning power of the class through the use of this asset.					
Week 18	Teach an introductory lesson on Making Meaning. Use it in mini-lessons throughout the week to begin to install the use of this asset within your students. Celebrate the new learning power of the class through the use of this asset.					
Week 19	Teach an introductory lesson on Summarizing. Use it in mini-lessons throughout the week to begin to install the use of this asset within your students. Celebrate the new learning power of the class through the use of this asset.					
Week 20	Teach an introductory lesson on Point of View. Use it in mini-lessons throughout the week to begin to install the use of this asset within your students. Celebrate the new learning power of the class through the use of this asset.					

S	M	T	W	T	F	S
Week 21	Teach an introductory lesson on Thoughtful Behavior. Use it in mini-lessons throughout the week to begin to install the use of this asset within your students. Celebrate the new learning power of the class through the use of this asset.					
Week 22	Teach an introductory lesson on Effective Expression. Use it in mini-lessons throughout the week to begin to install the use of this asset within your students. Celebrate the new learning power of the class through the use of this asset.					
Week 23	Teach an introductory lesson on Appropriate Courage. Use it in mini-lessons throughout the week to begin to install the use of this asset within your students. Celebrate the new learning power of the class through the use of this asset.					
Week 24	Teach an introductory lesson on Finishing Power. Use it in mini-lessons throughout the week to begin to install the use of this asset within your students. Celebrate the new learning power of the class through the use of this asset.					
Week 25	Teach an introductory lesson on Learning from Experience. Use it in mini-lessons throughout the week to begin to install the use of this asset within your students. Celebrate the new learning power of the class through the use of this asset.					

References and
Recommended Reading

Adams, M. J. (1989). Thinking skills curricula: Their promise and progress. *Educational Psychologist, 24* (1), 25–7.

Albee, G. W. (1980). A competency model must replace the deficit model. In L. Bond & J. Rosen (Eds.) *Competence and coping skills during adulthood,* (pp. 75–104). Hanover, NY: University Press of New England.

Allington, R., & Cunningham, P. (1996). *Schools that work: Where all children read and write.* New York: Addison-Wesley.

Amen, D. (1998). *Change your brain change your life.* New York: Random House.

Barell, J. (1999). Did you ask a good question today? In B. Presseisen (Ed.), *Teaching for Intelligence 1998* (pp. 97–105). Arlington Heights, IL: SkyLight.

Beasley, F. (1984). *An evaluation of Feuerstein's model for the remediation of adolescents' cognitive deficits.* Unpublished doctoral dissertation. University London.

Beck, A. (1976). *Cognitive therapy and the emotional disorders.* New York: Penguin.

Ben-Hur, M. (Ed.). (1994). *On Feuerstein's instrumental enrichment: A collection.* Arlington Heights, IL: Skylight.

Benson, H. (1996). *Timeless healing: The power and biology of belief.* New York: Fireside.

Beyer, B. (1983). Common sense about teaching thinking skills. *Educational Leadership 41*(3), 44–49.

Blades, J. (2000). *Action based learning: Linking movement to learning.* Paper presented at Eric Jensen's Learning Brain Expo 2000, San Diego, CA.

Bloom, B., Engelhart, M., Furst, E., Hill, W., & Kratwohl, D. (1956*). Taxonomy of educational objectives: Cognitive domain, Handbook 1.* New York: David McKay Co.

Brandt, R. (2000). Educators need to know about the brain. In *A. Costa (Ed.),
Teaching for intelligence 1999* (pp. 141–151). Arlington Heights, IL:
SkyLight.

Brandt, R. (1988). On teaching thinking : A conversation with Arthur Costa.
Educational leadership 45(7): 10–13.

Bransford, J., Brown, A., & Cocking, R. (Eds.). (1999). *How people learn: Brain,
mind, experience, and school.* Washington, DC: National Academy Press.

Burden, R. & Williams, M. (Eds.). (1998). *Thinking through the curriculum.*
London: Routledge.

Buzan, T. (1983). *Use both sides of your brain.* New York: E.P. Dutton.

Caine, G., & Caine, R. (1997). *Education on the edge of possibility.* Alexandria, VA:
Association for Supervision and Curriculum Development.

Caine, G., Caine, R., & Crowell, S. (1994). *Mindshifts: A brain-based process for
restructuring schools and renewing education.* Tucson, AZ: Zepher Press.

Carper, J. (2000). *Your miracle brain.* New York: HarperCollins.

Carter, R. (1998). *Mapping the mind.* Los Angeles: University of California Press.

Case, R. (1991). *The mind's staircase: Exploring the conceptual underpinnings of
children's thought and knowledge.* Hillsdale, NJ: Lawrence Erlbaum
Associates.

Case, R. (1992). The role of the frontal lobes in the regulation of cognitive
development. *Brain and Cognition, 20,* 51–73.

Costa, A. (Ed.) (1991). *Developing minds: Programs for teaching thinking (Vol. 1
& 2).* Alexandria, VA: Association of Supervision and Curriculum
Development.

Costa, A. (1991). *School as home for the mind.* Arlington Heights, IL: Skylight.

Costa, A., & Liebmann, R. (1997). *Process as content: Envisioning a renaissance
curriculum.* Thousand Oaks, CA: Corwin Press.

Csikszentmihalyi, M. (1990). *Flow: The psychology of optimal experience.* New
York: Harper & Row.

Campbell, L., & Campbell, B. (1999). *Multiple intelligences' and student achievement.* Alexandria, VA: Association for Supervision and Curriculum Development.

Darling-Hammond, L. (1999). Teacher learning that supports student learning. In B. Presseisen (Ed.). *Teaching for intelligence 1998.* (pp. 87–96). Arlington Heights, IL: SkyLight.

Das, J., Kar, B., & Parrila, R. (1996). *Cognitive planning: The psychological basis of intelligent behavior.* New Delhi, India: Sage.

Das, J., Naglieri, J., & Kirby, J. (1994). *Assessment of cognitive processes: The pass theory of intelligence.* Needham Heights, MA: Allyn & Bacon.

DeBray, R. (1990). Reviving thought processes in pre-adolescents: Toward a dynamic conception of intelligence: Is it possible to learn how to think? *International Journal of Cognitive Education and Mediated Learning,* 1(3), 211–219.

Dembo, M. (1991). *Applying educational psychology in the classroom (4th ed.).* New York: Longman.

Deming, W. (1994). *The new economics for industry, government, education (2nd ed.).* Cambridge, MA: MIT Press.

Duttweiler, P., & Robinson, N. (1999, Fall). *Part of the blueprint for standards-based reform is mission: Where is the foundation?* (Special Report, #2). Clemson, SC: Clemson University National Dropout Prevention Center.

Eggen, P., & Kauchak, D. (Eds.) (1994). *Educational psychology.* Upper Saddle River, NJ: Prentice-Hall.

Eisner, E. (1994). *Cognition and curriculum reconsidered.* New York: Teachers College Press.

Ellis, A., & Fouts, J. (1997). *Research on educational innovations.* Larchmont, NY: Eye on Education Publications.

Emerson, L. (1986). *Feuerstein's cognitive education theory and American Indian education.* Paper presented at the Mediated Learning Experience International Workshop, Jerusalem, Israel.

Erickson, H. (1998). *Concept-based curriculum and instruction.* Thousand Oaks, CA: Corwin Press.

Ferguson, M. (1987). *The aquarian conspiracy: Personal and social transformation in the 1980's.* Los Angeles: J.P. Tarcher.

Feuerstein, R., Feuerstein, R., & Gross, S. (1997). The learning potential assessment device. In D. Flanagan, J. Genshaft, & P. Harrison (Eds.), *Contemporary intellectual assessment* (pp. 297–311). New York: Guilford Press.

Feuerstein, R., Klein, P. S., Tannenbaum, A. J. (1991). *Mediated learning experience (MLE): Theoretical, psychosocial and learning Implications.* London: Freud.

Feuerstein, R., Miller, R., Hoffman, M. B., Rand, Y., Mintzker, Y., Jensen, M. R. (1981). Cognitive modifiability in adolescents: Cognitive structure and the effects of intervention. *Journal of Special Education, 15,* 269–287.

Feuerstein, R., Rand, Y., Hoffman, M. B. (1979*). The dynamic assessment of retarded performers: The learning potential assessment devise (LPAD) theory, instruments and techniques.* Baltimore: University Park Press.

Feuerstein, R., Rand, Y., Hoffman, M. B., Miller, R. (1980). *Instrumental enrichment: An intervention program for cognitive modifiability.* Baltimore: University Park Press.

Feuerstein, R., Rand, Y., Rynder, J. E. (1988). *Don't accept me as I am.* New York and London: Plenum Press.

Fisher, A., Murray, E., Bundy, A. (Eds.). (1991). *Sensory integration theory and practice.* Philadelphia: F. A. Davis Co.

Fogarty, R. (1997). *Brain compatible classrooms.* Arlington Heights, IL: Skylight.

Gardner, H. (1983). *Frames of mind.* New York: Bantam Books.

Gardner, H. (1998). Are there additional intelligences? The case for natural, spiritual and existential intelligences. In J. Kane (Ed.), *Education, information, and transformation.* Engelwood Cliffs, NJ: Prentice Hall.

Gardner, H. (1999). *The disciplined mind: What all students should understand.* New York: Simon & Schuster.

Gilg, J. (1990). *The use of mediated learning to enhance the educational effectiveness of school programs for high-risk youth. International Journal of Cognitive Education and Mediated Learning, 1*(1), 63–71.

260

Goleman, D. (1995). *Emotional intelligence: Why it can matter more than IQ.* New York: Bantam Books.

Gottman, J., & Silver, N. (1999). *The seven principles for making marriage work.* New York: Crown.

Greenberg, K. (1990). *Mediated learning in the classroom. International Journal of Cognitive Education and Mediated Learning 1,* 33–44.

Hannaford, C. (1995). *Smart moves.* Arlington, VA: Great Ocean.

Hawkins, D. (1998). *Power vs. Force.* Sedona, Arizona: Veritas Publishing.

Haywood, C., & Tzuriel, D. (Eds.) (1992). *Interactive assessment.* New York: Springer-Verlag.

Healy, J. (1990). *Endangered minds: Why our children don't think.* New York: Simon and Schuster.

Henner, M. (2001). *Healthy kids: Help them eat smart and stay active for life!* New York: HarperCollins.

Herrmann, N. (1995). *The creative brain (5th ed.)* Lake Lure, NC: The Ned Herrmann Group.

Hilliard, A. (1987). The learning potential assessment device and instrumental enrichment as a paradigm shift. *The Negro Educational Review, 38* (2-3), 200-208.

Jones, B., Palincsar A., Ogle, D., & Carr, E. (1987). *Strategic teaching and learning: cognitive instruction in the content areas.* Alexandria, VA: Association for Supervision and Curriculum Development.

Jones, M. (1998). *The thinker's toolkit.* New York: Three Rivers Press.

Kelley, R. (1998). *How to be a star at work.* New York: Random House.

Kessler, R. (2000). *The soul of education.* Alexandria, VA: Association for Supervision and Curriculum Development.

Klein, P. (1996). *Early interventions: A cross cultural application of a mediational approach.* New York: Garland Publishing.

Kozulin, A., & Kaufman, R., & Lurie, L. (1997). Evaluation of the cognitive intervention with immigrant students from Ethiopia. In A. Kozulin (Ed.), *The onthogeny of cognitive modifiability* (pp. 89–130). Jerusalem: ICELP.

Laughlan, F., & Elliott, J. (1998). Using dynamic assessment materials as a tool for providing cognitive intervention to children with complex learning difficulties. *Educational and Child Psychology, 14*(4), 137–148.

Lidz, C. (1991). *Practitioner's guide to dynamic assessment.* New York: Guilford Press.

Lindsay, G., & Thompson, D. (1997). *Values into practice in special education.* London: David Fulton.

Longo, P. (1999). *Distributed knowledge in the brain: Using visual thinking to improve student learning.* Paper presented at Piri's Learning and the Brain Conference 1999, Boston, MA.

Luria, A. (1960). *Cognitive development: Its cultural and social foundations* (M. Lopez-Morillas & L. Solotaroff, Trans.). Cambridge, MA: Harvard University Press.

Martin, D.S. (1984). *Can teachers become better thinkers?* Paper presented at annual meeting of the Association of Teacher Educators, New Orleans, LA.

Moye, V. (1997). *Conditions that support transfer.* Arlington Heights, IL: SkyLight.

Naglieri, J., & Das, J. (1997). *Das-Naglieri cognitive assessment system.* Itasca, IL: Riverside Publishing.

Ornstein, R., & Swencionis, C. (1990). *The healing brain: A scientific reader.* New York: Guilford.

Perkins, D. (1995). *Outsmarting IQ: The emerging science of learnable intelligence.* New York: The Free Press.

Perkins, D. (1992). *Smart schools: Better thinking and learning for every child.* New York: The Free Press.

Piaget, J. (1954). *The construction of reality in the child.* New York: Basic Books.

Piaget, J. (1977). *The development of thought: Equilibration of cognitive structures.* New York: Viking Press.

Presseisen, B. Z. (1985). *Unreadable lessons: Current and past reforms for school improvement.* Philadelphia: Falmer Press.

Presseisen, B. Z. (1986). *Critical thinking and thinking skills: State of the art definition and practice in public schools.* Philadelphia: Research for Better Schools.

Presseisen, B. Z. (1988). *At-risk students and thinking: Perspectives from research.* Washington, DC: A joint publication of the National Education Association and Research for Better Schools.

Ogle, D. (2000). Multiple intelligences and reading instruction. In A. Costa *Teaching for intelligence 1999.* Arlington Heights, IL: SkyLight.

Olivier, C., & Bowler, R. (1996). *Learning to learn.* New York: Fireside.

Ornstein, R., & Swencionis, C. (1990). *The healing brain: A scientific reader.* New York: Guilford.

Ornstein, R., & Thompson, R. (1984). *The amazing brain.* Boston: Houghton Mifflin.

Ratey, J. (2001). *A user's guide to the brain: Perception, attention, and the four theaters of the brain.* New York: Pantheon.

Resnick, L., & Klopfer, L. (1989). *Toward the thinking curriculum: Current cognitive research 1989 yearbook.* Alexandria, VA: Association for Supervision and Curriculum Development.

Richardson, A. (Ed.). (1997). *Canadian childhood in 1997.* Edmonton, Canada: Kanata Learning Co.

Roizen, M. (1999). *Realage: Are you as young as you can be?* New York: HarperCollins.

Roizen, M. (2001). *The realage diet: Make yourself younger with what you eat.* New York: HarperCollins.

Salema, M. & Valente, Maria. (1990). Learning to think: Metacognition in written composition. *International Journal of Cognitive Education and Mediated Learning, 1(2)*, 161–170.

Sapolsky, R. (1998). *Why zebras don't get ulcers: An updated guide to stress, stress-related diseases, and coping.* New York: Freeman.

Schlosser, E. (2001). *Fast food nation: The dark side of the all-American meal.* New York: Houghton Mifflin.

Secretary's Commission on Achieving Necessary Skills (SCANS). (1991). *What work requires of schools: A SCANS report for America 2000.* Washington, DC: U.S. Department of Labor.

Seligman, M. (1998). *Learned optimism: How to change your mind and your life.* New York: Simon & Schuster.

Senge, P. (2000) Systems change in education. In A. Costa, *Teaching for intelligence 1999* (pp. 3–16). Arlington Heights, IL: SkyLight.

Siegel, D. (1999). *The developing mind: Toward a neurobiology of interpersonal experience.* New York: Guilford.

Sousa, D. (1995). *How the brain learns.* Reston, VA: National Association of Secondary School Principals.

Schacter, D. (1996). *Searching for memory: The brain, the mind, and the past.* New York: Basic Books.

Sharron, E. (1987). *Changing children's minds: Feuerstein's revolution in the teaching of intelligence.* London, England: Souvenir Press.

Somer, E. (1995). *Food and mood: How the nutrients in food improve memory, energy levels, sleep patterns, weight management, and attitude.* New York: Henry Holt.

Stainback, S., & Stainback, B. L. (1989). *Educating all students in the mainstream of regular education.* New York: Paul H. Brookes Publishing.

Sternberg, R. (1997a). Intelligence and lifelong learning: What's new and how can we use it? *American Psychologist, 52,* 1134–1138.

Sternberg, R. (1997b). *Successful intelligence: How practical and creative intelligence determine success in life.* New York: Penguin.

Sternberg, R. (1997). What does it mean to be smart? *Educational Leadership, 54*(6), 20–24.

Sternberg, R. (1999). Schools should nurture wisdom. In B. Presseisen (Ed.). *Teaching for Intelligence 1998.* (pp. 55-82). Arlington Heights: SkyLight.

Sternberg, R., & Grigorenko, E. (Eds.). (1997). *Intelligence: Heredity and environment.* New York: Cambridge University Press.

Sternberg, R., & Spear-Swerling, L. (1996). *Teaching for thinking.* Washington, DC: American Psychological Association.

Sylwester, R. (1995). *A celebration of neurons: An educator's guide to the brain.* Alexandria, VA: Association of Supervision and Curriculum Development.

Tzuriel, D., Keniel, S., Zeliger, M., Friedman, A., & Haywood, H. (1998). Effects of the Bright Start program in kindergarten on use of mediated learning strategies and children's cognitive modifiability. *Child Development and Care, 143,* 1–20.

Vaughan, S. (1997). *The talking cure: Why traditional talking therapy offers a better chance for long-term relief than any drug.* New York: Henry Holt.

Vygotsky, L. (1978). *Mind in society.* Cambridge, MA: Harvard University Press.

Wenger, W., & Poe, R. (1996). *The Einstein factor: A proven new method for increasing your intelligence.* Rocklin, CA: Prima Publishing.

Wilson, D., & Greenberg, K. (2000). Learning to learn: The cognitive enrichment advantage approach. In A. Costa (Ed.), *Teaching for intelligence 1999* (pp. 285–296). Arlington Heights, IL: SkyLight.

Willett, W. (2001). *Eat, drink, and be healthy: The Harvard medical school guide to healthy eating.* New York: Simon & Schuster.

Wurtman, J. (1986). *Managing your mind and mood through food.* New York: Harper and Row.

About the Authors

Marcus Conyers
"The Brain Guy"

Marcus Conyers, international author and researcher, is a leading pioneer in translating implications of brain research into tools for boosting learning and teaching. He spent over 25 years in 35 countries developing BrainSMART, a research based system for boosting student achievement grounded in how neuroscience suggests the human brain naturally learns best.

Founder of BrainSMART Inc., Marcus has inspired millions by his appearances on more than 600 TV and radio shows around the world. He has authored 7 books including *BrainSMART Early Start with Dr. Lola Heverly, Radiant Health with Professor Brian Peskin, Speed Reading the Easy Way with Howard Berg, BrainSMART in the House: Learning for School - Learning for Life, Courageous Learners: Tools for Teachers of Students at Risk,* and *The BrainSMART Achievement Series with Dr. Donna Wilson.*

Marcus has taught BrainSMART to 30,000 teachers, students, corporate trainers, and university faculty around the world. The system has been chosen by the Florida Department of Education for a three year state wide "train the trainer" initiative for promoting dropout prevention. He is one of the most dynamic keynoters in education today.

Marcus presents BrainSMART at leading state, national, and international conferences including the following: *National Dropout Prevention Conference, Teaching for Intelligence, National At-Risk Conference, National Staff Development Council, National Association of Secondary School Principals, International Alliance for Learning, International Elementary School Consortium, The Mind Brain and the Learner Conference, Canadian Organization of Campus Activities,* and the *Texas Association of School Boards' Parent Learning Network.*

Marcus Conyers, BrainSMART Inc.
127 West Fairbanks Avenue #235
Winter Park, FL 32789
Phone (Toll Free): 1-866-SMART61
E-mail: marcus@brainsmart.com

Donna Wilson, Ph.D.

Donna Wilson, Ph.D., former chair of education at University of Detroit Mercy, led faculty to create current cognitive, innovative, and transformational field-based courses and programs. Her university expertise is featured in the SkyLight video distance education series *"Active Learning"*. A leader in the development of brain friendly learning systems grounded in cognitive education, Donna is a consultant and author specializing in the creation of learning and thinking schools. She has presented to thousands of educators and parents in all regions of the United States and in Canada, as well as sites internationally.

Donna has conducted research in applied cognitive education, health care, and reading with children. She is also author of several professional articles on educational change and cognitive education. Donna's other books include *Courageous Learners:Tools for Teachers of Students In At-Risk Situations, BrainSMART In The House:Learning for School Learning for Life, The BrainSMART Achievement Series* with Marcus Conyers, and *Mediated Learning In and Out of the Classroom Training Manual* with James Bellanca. Her work in professional development is also featured in SkyLight's *"Meet the Expert Series."*

Wilson has presented at leading state, national, and international conferences including the following: *American Educational Research Association, Teaching for Intelligence, International Association of Teachers of English as Second Language, National Dropout Prevention, National Association of School Psychologists, International Association of Cognitive Education, National Staff Development, National Association of Teacher Educators, International Alliance of Learning, Oklahoma State Legislature* and numerous other sites affiliated with professional as well as civic groups.

As a school psychologist and teacher, Donna received the *Outstanding Young Woman of the Year Award* in Oklahoma for accomplishments including community leadership to establish parent/school partnerships; developing a model for 100% employability for young people upon graduation; and developing best practices for students in at-risk situations. Donna was also recipient of a major grant awarded from BellSouth for production of an innovative teacher induction program for new teachers who work with a large number of poor students in rural areas. She has worked as a consultant in many schools, districts, and states including the following: *St. Louis; St. Tammany Parish, Louisiana; Chicago; Pine Grove, Pennsylvania; New York State; Detroit; Ft. Worth, Texas; Wilmington, Delaware; Orlando, Florida; Monroe County, Florida; New York City; Texas Association of School Boards; Marian County, West Virginia; Texas Education Association; Parent Learning Network; Dallas, Texas; Phoenix, Arizona; Norman, Oklahoma; and many others.*

Donna Wilson, BrainSMART Inc.
127 West Fairbanks Avenue #235
Winter Park, FL. 32789
Phone (Toll Free): 1-866-SMART61
Email: donna@brainsmart.com

BrainSMART, Inc.
Applying the Science of Learning
1800 Pembrook Drive, Suite 300
Orlando, FL 32810
(866) SMART61 Fax (407) 660-0012

Order Form

☐ Fax
PO No. _____
*(Required for fax orders -
include copy of PO with this form)*

Tax ID No. _____

☐ Mail *(include check, or must be
accompanied by PO)*

**To place a credit card order,
please visit our website at
www.brainsmart.com**

Bill To:

_____

_____

_____

_____

Ship To:

_____

_____

_____

_____

BrainSMART™ Books	Quantity	Price	
BrainSMART Thinking for Results	_____	39.00	_____
BrainSMART Strategies for Boosting Test Scores	_____	39.00	_____
Courageous Learners: Unleashing the Brain Power of Students from At-Risk Situations	_____	39.00	_____
BrainSMART In The House	_____	35.00	_____
Peak Performance: Radiant Health	_____	25.00	_____
BrainSMART Early Start	_____	39.00	_____
Shipping & Handling $6.00 per book.	_____	6.00	_____
Shipping for quantities over 5 books: 5% of price	_____	5%	_____

BrainSMART™ Teaching - Distance Learning Videos

Strategies Series
Episode 1 - The Body Brain System: Leaner Body Sharper Mind
Episode 2 - Gateways to Learning: Perception, .Senses, and Emotion
Episode 3 - Teaching to Strengths: How to R.E.A.D. and Reach Your Students
Episode 4 - Boosting Attention - Improving Metacognition
Episode 5 - Increasing Retention & Recall

Episode 6 - Teaching for Meaning	_____	$595	_____
60+ page Companion Study Guide	_____	$10	_____

Thinking for Results Series
Episode 1 -Introduction to Thinking for Results: Safer Schools
        and Higher Student Achievement
Episode 2 - Power of Practical Optimism
Episode 3 - Cultivating Cognitive Assets
Episode 4 - Cultivating Cognitive Assets: Curriculum Connections
Episode 5 - Thinking for Health

Episode 6 - How to Structure a Learning Environment: Fitness in the Thinking Lab	_____	$595	_____

BrainSMART™ Posters (Laminated)

5 Unit Poster Set BrainSMART Strategies	set of 5		
Building Great States, Making Meaning, Laser Sharp Attention, Tools for Transfer, 10 Pegs for Memory	_____	50.00	_____
* Regular postage included			
7 Unit Poster Set BrainSMART Thinking for Results	set of 7		
Metacognition: Driving My Brain, Making the Most of Time, Understanding Space, Self Regulation, Systematic Search, Planning, and Effective Expression			
* Shipping & Handling included	_____	75.00	_____

BrainSMART Hat	_____	10.50	_____
BrainSMART Whistle	_____	9.00	_____

Total: _____